Renting & letting

"Renting and letting a property requires a vast knowledge of rules and regulations for both landlords and tenants, yet many enter into the process with little preparation. To avoid rogue tenants and landlords and to make sure your rent is safe and that you don't end up losing your property, you must understand the dos and don'ts before you start as the rental process can happen in a matter of hours."

Kate Faulkner

About the author

Kate Faulkner is a consultant to residential property companies helping them communicate more clearly with tenants and buy-to-let investors. She also has first-hand experience of renting and letting property. Kate is the author of three other Which? books and runs www.designsonproperty.co.uk, which gives property market updates and creates new products and services to improve the renting and letting process.

Renting & letting

Kate Faulkner

Which? works for you

This book is for my family and friends, who are always there for me.

Which? Books are commissioned and published by Which? Ltd,
2 Marylebone Road, London NW1 4DF
Email: books@which.co.uk

Distributed by Littlehampton Book Services Ltd,
Faraday Close, Durrington, Worthing, West Sussex BN13 3RB

British Library Cataloguing in Publication Data
A catalogue record for this book is available from the British Library

First edition 2006. Second edition 2008. Third edition 2011. Fourth edition 2013.
ISBN: 978 1 84490 146 3

1 3 5 7 9 10 8 6 4 2

Author's acknowledgements
Big thanks to Sean and Emma Callery for their help, support and continued generosity; Bob Vickers, Kerenza Swift and Angela Newton; Sian Evans at Weightmans; Richard Grayson from Nicholsons; Mark Montgomery from 1st Property Lawyers; Andrew, Mike, Paul and Terry from Belvoir Lettings; Paul at Lindsays for help with Scotland; Paul Shamplina from Landlord Action; David from The Letting Network; The Deposit Protection Service, and Amanda from Designs on Property. The chart on page 23 is published courtesy of www.belvoirlettings.com.

Additional text by: Sean Callery
Printed and bound by Charterhouse, Hatfield

Essential Velvet is an elemental chlorine-free paper produced at Condat in Périgord, France, using timber from sustainably managed forests. The mill is ISO14001 and EMAS certified.

For a full list of Which? Books, please call 01992 822800, access our website at www.which.co.uk/books, or write to Littlehampton Book Services.

Contents

Introduction

Reports estimate that the demand for renting is going to increase by over a million homes by 2016. This is good news for landlords and for tenants there will be more homes to choose from, but rent may also be increase.

Since the credit crunch in 2007, renting and letting has experienced its share of ups and downs. For landlords, the value of property is likely to have dropped by up to 20 per cent or more. In the autumn of 2008, rents also fell by 5 per cent on average nationally, but in some areas where supply increased more than demand, rents fell by up to 20 per cent. So not only were property values down, rents were down too. The main driver for the increase in supply was people letting their homes when they couldn't sell them. So although the future looks bright for some landlords, others have had their homes repossessed. This has also impacted on tenants who have had to move out of the repossessed properties.

From a tenant's perspective, although it may be tough to get on the property ladder, renting offers flexible accommodation and increased mobility. Also, if anything goes wrong with the property, someone else picks up the bill to fix it. As a result, more people are moving into rented accommodation rather than buying a new home.

Why rent or let?

Rents tend to be less volatile than property prices as they usually keep in line with wage inflation – or deflation. So despite news headlines of 'rises' in rents throughout 2011, what actually happened was that rents were recovering from the falls in 2008. In many areas by 2012, rents were still lower than they were five years ago, so it's important not to take too much notice of news headlines on rents or house prices, but get to know what's actually happening in your local area.

Rents also vary less than house prices at a local level. So from a tenant's perspective, if you want to live in a nice house in a nice area, it's often cheaper to rent there than it is to buy. The downside is that you can only typically guarantee that you will have a home for six months. This is especially the case if you rent from someone who isn't a professional landlord and may look to sell their property as soon as the market picks up.

From a landlord's perspective, rent stability means you need to decide if you want to invest in buy-to-let properties to secure capital growth or for an income stream. Your decision can heavily influence where you buy (see pages 42–5).

Be informed

Since the credit crunch, rent and house prices in many areas are not following reported national averages. While in some areas rents may be rising, in others they may be falling or staying the same. So whether you are a landlord or a tenant, it is vital to find out from local letting agents what is actually happening in your area.

Rising rents

If rents are increasing, as a tenant make sure you have done your research, have your deposit ready and are clued up on letting rules and regulations before you look for a property. In some cases, when you visit, the agent or landlord may even have a credit card machine waiting for you to take a fee or a deposit. As a landlord, rising rents are good news, but don't take them for granted and make sure you keep your property well maintained to ensure you maximise your income.

Stable rents

If rents are stable, it typically means there are as many properties available to rent as there are people looking to find a property. As a tenant, you can therefore take your time a little more to choose a property. As a landlord, you need to make sure your property is more attractive than the competition so you can maximise your rent and keep your voids to a minimum.

Falling rents

If rents are on their way down, then it is worth finding the best property in the best area and holding onto it for as long as possible. A good landlord/letting agent will make sure the property remains in good condition, even if they are getting less rent. Poor landlords or letting agents will just do the minimum they have to and, as they aren't regulated, that may mean nothing!

If you are a landlord, the most important thing in a falling market is to ensure that your property is not left empty. You need to take what rent you can rather than aim to maximise the rent. In this way you limit any losses you would incur from the property being empty.

Professional bodies

National Landlords Association: www.landlords.org.uk
Residential Landlords Association: www.rla.org.uk

Letting agents

National Approved Letting Scheme: www.nalscheme.co.uk
Royal Institution of Chartered Surveyors: www.rics.org
The Property Ombudsman: www.tpos.co.uk
Association of Residential Letting Agents: www.arla.co.uk

An unregulated market

When a property is rented out privately, there are many safety regulations that have to be met. In addition, there has to be an agreement in place that highlights what the tenant's and landlord's rights and responsibilities are and what happens if a tenant wants to leave or a landlord wants the property back.

However, while there is plenty of legislation to make sure a tenant doesn't rent from a rogue landlord or letting agent, there is little enforcement of them. Few tenants take enough time to find out what is a legally let property, how to spot a good from a bad landlord and/or letting agent. As a tenant, it is therefore essential to understand not only your rights and responsibilities, but also that of your landlord and letting agent.

The same goes for a landlord. If you want to make a success out of letting property, you need to keep up to date with national and local rules and regulations.

Fortunately, as renting becomes more popular, governments, local authorities and organisations such as Which? and Shelter are looking at ways to make it as safe as possible for tenants to rent a property. This is particularly so in Northern Ireland, Scotland and Wales.

BE CAREFUL!

If you let property without assistance, you may find it difficult to keep within the law. If you try to let without declaring the extra income and Capital Gains Tax or complying with the rules and regulations, the chances of getting caught are increasing as the Government and local councils are clamping down on rogue landlords.

How this book helps

Due to a lack of regulation and enforcement of the rules, this book is essential for both landlords and tenants to understand how to work together successfully. From a landlord's perspective, it helps to explain how to pick the right area and property to invest in for your circumstances and how to make sure you let your property successfully and to the right tenant.

For tenants, this book explains how to spot a good landlord, how to avoid bad letting agents and how to make sure you rent a property that is legally let.

Crucially, all the legal aspects of letting and renting a property are explained, including assessing legal letting documents. It also informs you about the additional resources you need throughout your letting and renting experience. These include the trade associations and letting organisations that are essential to know about and turn to for help and advice just in case things go wrong. Read on and learn how to rent or let a property as successfully as possible.

Letting and renting

There are many reasons why people let out and rent property. This chapter looks at the main ones before delving deeper into the different types of rent that are available to prospective landlord and tenant alike.

Why let?

Approximately 15% of UK housing stock is rented out. Although this is expected to rise to 20 per cent by 2020, it is still far lower than the average of 30 per cent in the rest of Europe.

The vast majority of the properties are let by private landlords, and the market is now a national industry that splits into accidental landlords, people who are investing to add to their pension and those that make letting their business.

In a market where the rent is determined by the number of rooms, size matters. Most rented properties are small: a third of privately rented properties are flats and the remainder are mainly terraced or semi-detached houses. Demand is rising, partly due to the property prices over the last 10 years rising more than wages, partly due to a 'lifestyle' choice of our younger generation.

Over 4.8 million properties are let in the private sector with 47 per cent of 20 to 24-year-olds renting. When asked, 19 out of 20 16 to 19-year-olds expect renting to expand at the expense of home ownership. Many are professional single people or couples who either can't or don't want to buy into the property market and value the sense of freedom that comes with renting: if they want to move on, they can do so quickly and easily. Other factors driving tenant demand are increasing number of students and demand from first-time buyers unable to get a foot on the housing ladder. Increased immigration into the UK following the accession of the eastern European states has also had an impact in certain areas in the UK.

> **'Rented properties are in high demand: an uncertain economy makes renting a more flexible option.'**

The pluses and minuses

Over many years, property has proved so far to be a sound investment: prices have risen over time, in many cases far out performing what can be earned from a deposit account or equity investment. Letting offers a rental income plus the benefit of any growth in the property value.

However, prices can fall as well as rise (as we have seen since 2007) and the landlord is responsible for the maintenance of the property and has to find tenants willing to rent it or pay someone else to do this. It is important to view property investment as a long-term business investment, not a get-rich-quick scheme. In the main, a higher percentage of the earnings is from the rise in value, as opposed to the profit made on the monthly rent. The introduction of buy-to-let mortgages has encouraged more people into the letting market. These specialist deals are designed for those buying property expressly to let out to tenants (see pages 46–7). There are just under 1.5 million buy-to-let mortgages in the UK.

BE CAREFUL!

A property will tie up your money for some period of time, and unlike shares, you can't just decide to sell one day: you will have to consider your agreement with the tenant, and you are likely to need to produce an Energy Performance Certificate and then hope there is a buyer out there willing to pay the price you want!

Dreams of yield

The key word for landlords is yield: how much the property is earning for them. Yield can be calculated in lots of different ways, but in its simplest form, it is the total amount of rent, minus running costs, divided by how much the property cost. So a £145,000 property with annual rent of £16,000 that costs £1,500 a year to run will bring in £14,500 income. Divide this figure by the value of the property produces 0.1, which, expressed as a percentage (multiply by 100), is a yield of 10 per cent.

£16,000 – £1,500 = £14,500

£14,500 ÷ £145,000 = 0.1

0.1 x 100 = 10%

The reason it is really important to calculate yield is because it allows you to compare the returns from property to money left in the bank or invested elsewhere. The average yield in the UK varies from 5 to 6 per cent but can be more depending on the type of let and length of ownership.

Make sure that before you commit your hard-earned cash to buy to let you discuss your options with an **independent financial**

'Work out the potential yield – it might be better to invest your money elsewhere.'

For more information on yield and how to work out your return on investment, see pages 42–5 and 115–26. Reference: Keynote Research.

Jargon buster

Independent financial adviser (IFA) Someone trained in the complexities of financial management. Always check that anyone you speak to is regulated by the Financial Services Authority (FSA): www.fsa.gov.uk (FCA from 2013, see www.fsa.gov.uk/about/what/reg_reform/fca).
Yield How much your property is earning.

adviser (IFA) – it may be that you can get better returns from other investments, avoiding the associated administration and risk of buy to let altogether.

In summary, before you jump into buy to let, make sure you plan a realistic figure on the yield you can achieve – for more information, see pages 42–5.

Burst pipes and paperwork

Being a landlord is not easy. There are an enormous number of legal and safety checks to undertake, a lot of administration to keep on top of, and, of course, part of the role involves dealing with people, which brings its own complications. In addition, when a pipe bursts or a boiler goes cold, you get the call and need to sort out the problem fast. You will certainly need to set aside several hours a month to deal with administration and problems: one survey found the average was 12 hours a month – that is a day and a half of working time. Of course, much of this work can be done outside office hours, but that means it will eat into your leisure and family time unless you use a letting agent to do it for you.

Are you right for the role?

Not everyone makes a good landlord. You need to be:

- **Well organised** to deal with all the paperwork.
- **Prepared to get your hands dirty** doing routine maintenance.
- **Fit enough** to shift beds and wardrobes.
- **Good at dealing** with people.

FSA change of name

In 2013, the Financial Services Authority (FSA) is being disbanded and replaced with the Financial Conduct Authority (FCA). Its job is to protect consumers, enhance the integrity of the UK financial system and promote effective competition in the interests of consumers. It will also maintain a register of all the authorised financial firms and approved individuals.

Supporting cast

A landlord needs a strong supporting cast of trusted trades people such as a plumber, carpenter and electrician, plus possibly someone to help with administration such as inventories and checking regulations (so you'll know when your gas or electrical safety certificate expires, for example). A good letting agent should be able to help here (see pages 68–71). Without such back up, dealing with the inevitable problems can be stressful and expensive.

- **Able to handle the responsibility** regarding the legal regulations that come with the role.
- **Equipped** with a dependable business head.

If this doesn't sound like you, you probably shouldn't become a landlord, or you need to pay other people to deal with the hassle, which will eat into your income.

BE CAREFUL!
A number of companies run courses on property investment. These tend to be over-priced and over-hyped. Much of the information given is widely available elsewhere at a fraction of the cost. If you are interested, sign up for any free courses but don't be sucked into paying over the odds for the follow-ups, and don't take your cheque book or other form of payment so that you can't be hurried into a purchase by a hard sell.

Why be a landlord?

Most of the time, the answer is very simple: money. Letting to tenants provides a regular income while you still benefit from any rise in value of the property itself. It is a form of investment where you have more control than collections of stocks and shares, and can influence the rise in value by modernising and operating efficiently. You can also monitor how well your investment is doing (see page 42).

There are other benefits, too. There is the satisfaction of providing a service to others (how would students manage their accommodation needs without landlords?) and, for some, letting a room at home is a source of companionship. If you are interested in the property market, you can enjoy the stimulation of researching market conditions and viewing properties without the emotional complications that are inevitable when looking for a home for yourself.

Do some research

Talk to as many people as you can to find out if property investment is for you: it's a hard-nosed business that doesn't suit everybody. A good place to start researching life as a landlord is the website of the National Association of Landlords or the Residential Landlords Association (see below). The local authorities may also run local landlord accreditation schemes and events which are worth attending.

'Letting to tenants provides a guaranteed regular income for a landlord, and you can also benefit from any rise in value of the property itself.'

For landlord organisations visit **www.rla.org.uk** and **www.landlords.org.uk**.

Other ways to make money from property

You may have great faith that property prices will always continue to rise in the long term, but lack the commitment necessary to be a landlord. If so, there are a number of other routes to property investment.

Investing in syndicates

A syndicate is a group of people who own property together while paying a management company to run it and deal with the tenants and maintenance. Syndicates generally operate more than one property, and are often able to negotiate discounts on property purchase by buying in bulk (for example, purchasing a whole block of flats rather than one unit). This allows you to get involved in the property market at a lower initial cost and can help spread the risk. It is important that you seek professional advice from an independent financial adviser or solicitor specialising in property syndicates before considering this type of property ownership.

Property funds

These are organisations that buy, sell and manage property, in which you can invest. You have little say in the day-to-day running of the business, which is conducted according to an agreed prospectus. You can join a property fund through an independent financial adviser. Funds are regulated by the FSA (FCA from 2013, see page 12).

Renovating for profit

This is hands-on development for those who know the market and have the skills or contacts to improve a property quickly and sell it on. It is a tough route during a recession when property prices don't rise. These investors are often responsible for bringing semi-derelict or uninhabitable properties back into occupation.

Trading property

For those who know what they are doing and have the time and expertise to seek out undervalued or unwanted properties, perhaps make a few changes or improvements, such as obtaining planning permission for an extension, once value is added, it is possible to trade on at a profit.

Buying 'off plan'

The buyer purchases unbuilt property from a developer, hoping to sell it on at a profit after it is completed. The investment is highly risky in a static/falling property market.

It's your pension

Some people are concerned that they may not have enough invested to pay a nice bonus for retirement, and decide that by letting out property they can ensure that they receive an income while holding on to the equity of the rising value of their bricks and mortar. Few landlords make a lot of money from rental income: the bulk of their profit is gained through cashing in on the rising value of the properties they let. While property prices went up from the late 1990s to 2007, they fell by 20 per cent or more in the following years, and it is vital to allow for periods when the property is empty and you are not receiving any income. As always, when making crucial decisions about your future finances, it makes sense to get advice from an IFA.

Room to let

One of the ways in which people let property is by renting out a room in their own house. The reasons why you might choose to do this include:

- **To help pay** the mortgage or for extra income.
- **For company,** to combat the loneliness of living on your own, maybe after the children have fled the nest or after being widowed or divorced.
- **As a way of staying** in a much loved residence that would otherwise be too big.
- **Because you have the space** and feel it is the right thing to do to share it.

You may be able to offer some self-contained accommodation, such as a granny flat with its own bathroom and kitchen.

Sometimes the arrangement begins informally as a way of helping out a friend who needs a room for a short time. If you want to try out such an arrangement but do not want to enter into long-term commitments, you could try:

- **Local churches,** which often have links with groups in other parts of the country and may know of someone looking for a local room.
- **English language teaching schools.** There are many of these around the country, mainly based in cities and some towns, where students come from abroad to attend a course for a set period and need somewhere to stay.
- **Local companies** or other large employers, who might be taking on someone based at another location, perhaps as a temporary arrangement.

For more information on the different ways to make money out of property go to **www.propertychecklists.co.uk** and the *Which? Essential Guide: Property Investor's Handbook.*

Relocating or can't sell your own home

Another reason you might opt to let out your property is if you need to move or work away, possibly abroad, and do not want to sell your home. Letting out your home allows you to return to it when it is convenient for you to live in it again, while still covering the cost of owning a property. The downside is that, unlike other properties, this is your home and you have emotional ties to it. You may not feel comfortable with the idea of others living in it, and the inevitable wear and tear that goes with occupancy may feel like an intrusion when it is not your children's shoes that scuffed the paintwork. You may also be moved onto a buy-to-let mortgage, which attracts higher charges.

Working away from home

In today's job market, change happens fast. You might take on a temporary contract for, say, six months in another part of the country, or be offered a job elsewhere with the prospect of changing your conditions of work to do more from home, or from a base nearer to it. You may take a job elsewhere but want to maintain the equity of your current home, or keep your children attending a school where they are happy. There are many circumstances in which it makes sense to take on a flat near work but keep hold of your family home, even if you can only be there at weekends. You might then choose to rent out a spare room in the flat, thus improving its security by having someone living there all the time, and offsetting some of your own costs. The tenant gets a good deal because they will probably have the place to themselves when they most want it, at the weekend.

First-time landlord

Don't be afraid to ask a local specialist letting agent (not an agent that wants to sell you property too!) for advice before you start. They are likely to want to help because they'll be aware you might decide to market or manage the property through them. Look in local paper advertisements and ask letting agents for their rental lists to get an idea of local demand and prices. See also pages 68–71.

'You might decide to let out your property if you need to move for work and don't want to sell your home.'

Your student children need a roof over their heads

One factor that has prompted a number of people to take the plunge into letting is the high costs of student accommodation at a time when further education is already expensive. Buying a property near the university your

Case study Mr and Mrs James

Mr and Mrs James had just moved up to Lincolnshire having lived and worked around London for ten years. The plan was that Mrs James would buy and renovate property, some to sell and some to let, building up a property portfolio over the years. Unfortunately, the plan went pear-shaped when Mr James landed his dream job - back down south in Reading.

The cost to rent a room in Reading was £400-£500 a month and there were no guarantees that Mrs James could stay whenever she needed to work down south. The cost of property was much more than in Lincolnshire, with the cheapest properties being flats around £140,000 rather than a two-bed property for £70-£80,000!

A compromise was reached when Mrs James found a two-bedroom flat in need of renovation - in a good area in Reading - for sale for £135,000. The property was part of a housing association block of flats, and so there would always be a limited number of the flats available for private purchase, and therefore likely to always be a high demand for the flat when it came to sell.

However, the flat needed work, with a new bathroom, painting, new carpets and a good clean! To check what other work was required, the Jameses requested a property survey and a gas and electric survey to be done. The cost of the surveys were around £600. However, they found that the property needed a stopcock putting in to allow separation of the water supply from the rest of the block of flats and problems with the electrics that needed doing. The result was that the surveys helped to reduce the cost of the property by several thousand pounds, and offering a quick purchase, the property was actually bought for £125,000.

The work required cost just over £3,000, but the low purchase cost and the renovation to a good standard, fitting the tenant's room with a new desk and bed, trendy curtains and bedding, the room was let within a week of finishing the work for a full 12 months. The low price paid for the property meant that the room rent could always be set at lower than anyone else in the area, ensuring no problems re-letting and no voids. Free broadband was also thrown in as an incentive to secure a 12-month let.

As a result, instead of paying out £400-£500 a month on renting a room during the week, with no flexibility and certainly no chance of capital growth, the flat costs the Jameses much less than this every month as they gain rent from the other room and they have already made a capital gain on the property of over £20,000!

son or daughter attends means they won't have to pay any rent if you choose not to charge them. You may well be able to let out other rooms in the property, and will be confident that at least one of the tenants has your interests at heart, so the property should be treated fairly well. Of course, you could still be the landlord and will have to shoulder the legal and practical responsibilities that this entails.

Depending on who you are planning to rent out your property to, you will need to decorate and furnish it appropriately. See pages 22-34 for ideas on what you should be thinking about.

> **'You may be able to let out other rooms in the property, and be confident that at least one of the tenants has your interests at heart, so the property should be treated fairly well.'**

You inherited property

Many people inherit property from their parents. They may choose to move in to it themselves, or to sell it. However, it may not be easy to market or they may be reluctant to let go of what may be a much-loved property that houses many memories, or prefer to see it as an investment. In such cases letting is an option.

You want a holiday home

Buying a second property as a holiday home is a popular choice for many who wish to combine property investment with pleasure. The advantages of this arrangement are that you have ready access to your holiday accommodation, but cover its costs through letting it to other occupants during the holiday season. If you decide not to holiday at it one year, you can rent it out instead. You may decide to limit the renting to friends and family, which may make you very popular within your social circle but won't necessarily earn as much. Buying a holiday home to let out is an excellent way of establishing a foothold in a new area, perhaps with a view to retiring there.

A disadvantage is that the property may only attract interest during the holiday period and could stand empty for half of the year while you still have to pay the mortgage and upkeep. There is also the hassle of advertising for and dealing with holiday renters, although you can pay an agency to do this. Also, the holiday home is likely to be some distance from where you live, so you will not be able to deal with on-site problems quickly or easily. You'll need to do your sums and your business plan carefully if you plan to treat a holiday home as an investment.

You should consider whether to take on short- or long-term lets for your property. The advantages and disadvantages of both these types of let are described on pages 22–34.

Why rent?

Renters will include prospective first-time buyers trying to save for a deposit, but could also include people who have sold a property but have not found the dream home they are seeking.

In such a situation, renting makes a lot of sense: it gives them a chance to see what it is like living in an area where they may buy and to see what facilities and schools are like. They can then make an offer on a property as a cash buyer, rather than someone with a property chain dragging along behind them.

Another trend is for older people who choose to rent in the later part of their lives so that their outgoings are predictable and they can live within a set budget, possibly having sold the house that they owned.

There will, of course, also be some free spirits who choose to rent, preferring the flexibility it offers compared to that or living as an owner-occupier. They benefit from not being responsible for the maintenance of the property, so they can plan their finances very well because all the other costs related to accommodation (rent and bills) are predictable.

'Choosing to rent rather than take on a mortgage can provide a flexible lifestyle.'

Temporary accommodation

Another reason to rent is if your job moves to a different part of the country, perhaps temporarily, or that you are not confident will be a permanent arrangement. It makes sense to take a room or a small flat rather than go through the financial and emotional hassle of buying a property that you may need to sell in the near future. If you are considering moving to a new area, renting for six months to see what it is really like is an investment in your quality of life: if you find out that you don't like the area, you can move to another one far more easily than if you had bought property.

Two other groups of people that require temporary accommodation are students who are unlikely to be able to afford a property to buy, often go to college away from home, returning for holidays.

Many people don't think about taking a holiday cottage as rental accommodation, but it is, in its truest form, going away for a few weeks and staying in a property by the sea or a remote area of the country, or abroad.

The advantage of renting temporarily is that it can be a safer bet in times of economic uncertainty. If you invest in a property when prices were high, a fall in the market – as happened post the credit crunch – can mean you lose money on your investment, whereas rental prices are typically less volatile.

However, the disadvantage of renting in a rising property market is that you are not getting any return for your money apart from a roof over your head. Rent payments are considered as 'dead' money, while the price of the property you might eventually want to buy will go up, possibly out of your range.

Buy or rent?

It's difficult to know whether now is a good time to buy or even sell up and rent instead. It depends on your own personal and financial circumstances. There are various ways to calculate whether it's better to buy or rent:

1. Look out for 'buy or rent' indices such as at www.zoopla.co.uk/rentbuy/.
2. Use an online calculator to help you work out which is better over a number of years. For example, go to: www.letlink.co.uk/letting-library/tools-resources/buying-vs-renting-calculator.html.html.
3. Work out the costs of renting versus the costs of putting money into a property, the maintenance and the monthly owning costs over the same time period.

Who are you going to live with?

It is important to decide from the start whether you are just looking for accommodation for yourself or with others. Some people thrive on living on their own, others find it lonely. If you don't have a live-in partner, you could still look for two-bedroom properties with a friend or relative.

Advantages

- Self-contained two-bedroom properties are more cost effective to rent than those with one bedroom.
- You've got someone to share the hassle and the bills with.
- It might be more companionable than living alone.

Disadvantages

- Sharing a kitchen or bathroom with others can be tricky if they use your things or don't clean up after themselves.
- It is likely to be noisier – and many flats have poor sound insulation anyway, so someone else's life can intrude on your own.
- If you don't get on well, shared accommodation can be lonely and stressful, emotionally and financially.
- You might not like their friends, and resent the occasions when they visit.

What's your market?

As with any business, if you are planning to let property, it is essential to identify what your target market is, and ensure that your product suits their needs. You will need to do this before you buy, convert or decorate your property.

Short-term lets

Short-term lets are between one week and three months and are furnished. The rent usually includes charges for utilities, with the tenant expected to deal with the cost of the landline telephone (if used).

The number of tenants requiring short-term lets is rising as employers increasingly expect their staff to be mobile and to work for short stretches in different locations.

From the landlord's point of view, short-term lets are more work because the property must be in immaculate condition at all times and there is the ongoing need to market it for the next vacant period. In addition to higher set-up and maintenance costs, insurance premiums can be higher. However, rents are significantly higher and in the right location (usually city centres) a short-term let offers a better yield than a long-term one. Typical short-term lets are company and holiday lets.

Company lets

A company, or corporate, let is when you have a contract with a firm to accommodate their employees as tenants. It can pay very well, but requires properties of a very high (and therefore costly) standard. Senior executives sometimes have a working routine of being in one location for two days then moving to another region, but prefer the familiarity of a house or flat to the anonymity of hotel rooms. Beware that corporations may suddenly decide to relocate and no longer require property or even run out of cash to pay you. If you go for this market, make sure there is more than one suitably large firm in the area. Hospitals and universities are other organisations that sometimes require short-term, high-quality accommodation.

Typical locations

Obviously, the employee needs to be within easy reach of his or her workplace. Those without families are likely to prefer city-centre locations near shops and leisure facilities. Those with families

---

If you are a tenant in a short-term let, you have less security that in a long-term let (see pages 28–34). For more information on the legal position of tenants see pages 128–34 and 136–56.

Risk level

This is a general assessment of the level of risk of the buy-to-let market taking into consideration risks such as default on rent, damage to property and the likelihood of taking out legal proceedings.

Type of tenancy	**Average yield** (gross)	**Estimated risk level** (5 = high)
Company	5.5%	2
Professional	5.5%	3
Social	5.5%	1-2
Holiday let	5-10%	3-4
Student	6-10%	4
Houses in multiple occupation	8-15%	5

tend to go for suburban or rural locations with good transport links, preferably near a park. Tenants are likely to be professionals and will have high expectations of local schools if they have a family with them. For those from abroad, an international school within easy reach could be important.

Lets can be long or short term, and often include a charge for water, gas and electricity so that the client does not have to deal with setting up utility bills.

What you need to provide

An executive with no family or one who stays in the accommodation only during the working week is going to want a one- or two-bedroomed property with roomy living space. Families need more bedrooms, bathrooms and living space, a well-equipped utility room, and a garden suitable for children. Secure car parking is essential. The tenants will expect high quality televisions and viewing packages and hi-fi equipment, broadband access and a well-planned kitchen. Furniture should be modern and stylish. At the top end, corporate clients expect luxuries such as Egyptian cotton sheets and limestone bathrooms. Long-term professional tenants may prefer to come with their own furniture, but since they are likely to have vacated their own family home, may also wish you to provide it. Decoration should be elegant (no strong colours) with accessories such as antiques or artwork. Some corporate tenants will expect a maid and a laundry/garden service.

The tenant's take

As a tenant in accommodation recommended by (and possibly paid by) your employer, you'll expect high-standard furnishings and fittings and excellent security to reflect the premium rent being charged. You'll expect to be able to move in straightaway with the minimum of fuss, and know that someone from your firm or relocation agency has vetted the property thoroughly if you can't do so. You may want to arrange for a cleaner to visit regularly.

How to find tenants

- **Letting agents:** You may well have to go through letting agents (see pages 68–71) because companies tend to work with other professionals. However, it might be worth contacting human resource departments of large organisations – you'll save a big fee. They may arrange lettings themselves, especially for staff coming from abroad, or they may provide the employee with a budget and contacts. You may be able to advertise quite cheaply in the company newspaper or intranet.
- **Relocation firms** specialise in helping executives move to new posts. The ideal scenario is when a company takes out a let itself and simply sublets to its staff: you get a guaranteed premium rent without the hassle of finding new tenants or the dreaded void periods. However, try to limit tenant turnover as it can be disruptive, and carry out an inventory check with each changeover. For a local relocation firm, see www.arp-relocation.com.

BE CAREFUL!

You must take out specialist buildings and contents insurance on your holiday home (see pages 75-6): a standard household policy will not be suitable. Your policy should include public liability cover in case someone suffers injury or damage on the property.

Are you sure?

Although holiday lets can attract higher rent than residential lets, especially in high season, there are significant marketing, administration and managing costs. Using the property for your own breaks will reduce the income you receive, and you will probably have to visit regularly to check on its condition, while arranging repairs from a distance can be a nightmare. Finally, you can buy a lot of holidays for the cost of a house or flat! However, you will benefit from any rises in the property market and if you attract a full complement of bookings, you will generate a sizeable income.

Serviced apartments and 'apart hotel' lets

This is where you buy into the ownership of a hotel room or serviced apartment within a hotel or block. Although the rental returns can be good, your ability to sell it on is limited as these are usually for cash buyers only. Typically, these investments are based in international cities, such as London or New York, and you receive a percentage of the income generated from their use. Sometimes you are allocated a set number of days per annum that you can use the room for free.

As the income generated from hotels and serviced apartments is higher than from a standard buy to let, if they are well utilised, your average rental return can be a lot a higher. However, you need ready cash to invest as you can't borrow for these investments. This means that the potential selling market, when you cash in to make profit, may be non-existent.

Holiday lets

It sounds perfect: buy a property somewhere you enjoy visiting (and perhaps plan to retire to), use it when you like, and get it to pay for itself the rest of the time by running it as a holiday let. In reality, a lot of landlords operating holiday lets are glad to break even in this competitive and labour-intensive market. However, this is an expanding market: more than 4 million people rent cottages and holiday apartments every year, and self-catering holidays are increasingly popular.

Most holiday lets occur during the period of about 20–30 weeks covering late spring, summer and early autumn, but city properties are a likely bet all year round, and there can be high demand at Christmas and New Year. Standard lets are by the week, but weekend and mid-week breaks are popular, again especially in cities.

Typical locations

Obviously there are hotspots such as the Lake District, seaside resorts and major cities, such as London, York and Edinburgh, but the market for holiday lets is wide ranging. Pretty rural or seaside settings are extremely attractive, and a site close to shops and with good transport links is likely to attract valuable repeat bookings.

City properties should be as near the centre as possible, and certainly with good transport links. Elsewhere, the most attractive holiday lets are those that are conveniently situated among the local attractions, rather than on the edge of a popular region. A rural location might look attractive, but it could be vulnerable to burglars because it will be left unattended,

Can you hear the crowd?

One potentially lucrative sector in the letting market is short-term lets near major events such as sports tournaments. For example, houses located near the annual tennis championship in Wimbledon are much sought after by players and others attending. They expect high quality accommodation and good parking facilities. Privacy is a priority so you would have to move out - but the payback is the very high rent you can charge. Contact the organisers of the event to see what demand is like and to be added to their accommodation list, or seek advice from local letting agencies.

When you are calculating how much income you might earn from holiday lets, don't forget to allow for the potentially longer periods when the property will be empty. For more information on calculations, see pages 42–5.

and is likely to be equipped with attractive, portable equipment. You need a good burglar alarm.

Holiday lets are a quick turnaround business where the property needs to be freshened up between lets of a week or two, so either you will need to be on hand as a regular commitment, or you will need to find someone to do it for you: you can't run it yourself properly from a distance.

There are strict rules as to what constitutes a furnished holiday let, explained on page 121. From 6 April 2012 holiday lets must be in the UK or EEA (European Economic Area), furnished, available for letting for at least 210 days a year and commercially let (not at cheap rates to family and friends) for at least 105 days a year, with the lets not exceeding 31 days.

Helpful advice

Put together a handbook about the property with notes on how the hot water system works, when rubbish should be put out, and contact details if there is a problem. Include an inventory of all equipment provided, with a polite request for any broken items to be replaced and any damage or faults notified

In addition, put together a separate folder containing local information, such as shops, attractions and emergency contacts, such as the doctor. A visitor's book allows guests to leave their own suggestions and may provide you with useful feedback.

What you need to provide

The biggest market is for two- or three-bedroom properties that can sleep a family of four or five – so one bedroom should have twin beds. Decoration need not be as neutral as for residential properties: visitors will appreciate a cosy, warm atmosphere with plenty of pictures on the walls. The beds in particular should be of high quality – visitors are unlikely to want to return to a property where they slept badly.

The accommodation must be furnished like a normal property, including linen and towels (some landlords charge extra for these). You'll need to provide a television and a viewing package, video and DVDs. Provide heaters if there is no central heating, and have a cupboard with extra duvets and blankets. Guests will also expect a washing machine. The kitchen should be well equipped with crockery, cooking equipment and utensils, a microwave and a dishwasher. Many people like to have a radio in the kitchen, and possibly a television. Handling furnishings for holiday lets is different to other letting: you'll need to change bedding more often, for example, but general wear and tear is lower as people tend to be out a lot during their stay.

For changeover day (Friday or Saturday) you will need to undertake or arrange an inventory check, change of linen and towels, renew soap and toilet rolls, plus a clean up. It is kind to provide a welcome tray of tea, coffee, milk and biscuits, plus maybe a bottle of wine.

How to find tenants

- **Independent letting:** Around half of UK rented holiday homes are let independently rather than through agents. Contact the local tourist office and ask what information they need for you to be added to their list of holiday lets. Many people look for holiday lets on the internet and the easiest way to put yourself forward is to add your property to a local or specialist holiday homes directory (the regional tourist board should have a list of properties, or try www.holidaylettings.co.uk or www.homeaway.co.uk.
- **Create your own website,** but only try this if you know what you are doing, as it must look professional.
- **Use a specialist letting agent,** for marketing or managing the property. This will take up a sizeable chunk of your income (they'll charge a percentage of income, possibly up to 49 per cent for a full service), but they should be able to fill your bookings list more efficiently than you can. You obviously have the option of taking a limited number of private (possibly repeat) bookings separately and informing the agent of any weeks that are not available.
- **Let to friends and family.** This is a good option but beware of doing this for long periods at discounted rents as it could affect your tax position (see page 121).

The tenant's take

If you book early (at least six months ahead for the summer), you will be spoilt for choice. Once you have selected your choice of region(s) you can find details of holiday lets via local tourist offices, or via the internet, where you can usually check availability very easily. Smokers and guests with pets will have to shop around as some landlords do not welcome them. Watch out for variations on changeover days, especially if you are transferring from one holiday let to another in a twin location break: some go for Friday, others for Saturday.

Tenants are also becoming a target for criminals. 'Legitimate' properties to let are advertised online with deposits sent electronically. Then, on arrival, there either is no property or it is being rented by someone else! Never send money unless you have an independent reference from a licensing board, tourist bureau. Also, ask to speak to the company's legal representative, tax adviser or accountant.

Long-term lets

Long-term lets are typically for people who want to rent a home to live in. Long-term letting is a minimum of six months, but the average length of time that a tenant now stays in a home, according to ARLA, is nearly 20 months.

Student lets

The student let market is very active, highly competitive, and growing fast. The number of undergraduates has risen by 30 per cent in the last decade, but university and college accommodation provision has not, and about half of all students rent in the private sector. Tenants tend to be aged around 20, so have a young lifestyle that does not always match that of their neighbours – which does not always make them ideal tenants. When marketing to students, remember their parents will be keen that the accommodation meets their expectations (and they may well be paying for it) so you are 'selling' to them too.

However, the future of student housing following funding issues regarding loans relies on the success of the university or institution to attract students. It is essential to carry out detailed research on which streets students want to live on and where the experts expect student investment will be successful as opposed to oversupplied.

The bulk of students often only want accommodation during the academic year, which runs from late September to mid June, although some courses run longer than this. Therefore, there will be a void period in July and August for which you may choose to try to charge a holding fee. Many universities and colleges run separate courses during this summer period and the accommodation office should be able to advise you what demand is like during this time. It is also worth knowing that students are exempt from paying Council Tax.

A high number of students come to study from overseas. They often make very good tenants because they usually behave very responsibly and tend to stay in

BE CAREFUL!

If letting rooms to students you may need a licence. See page 30-33 for more details.

the property over holiday periods. They may be able to pay up-front for accommodation, but properties need to be bespoke to their needs, for example warm and have specific kitchen items.

A major decision to be made is whether to let your rooms separately or as a multiple tenancy. Letting rooms individually might bring in more rental income, but you will also have to deal with more administration as each tenant has a separate agreement. The other issue is whether the tenants get on with each other: domestic tension can result in people moving out or arguing over bills, both of which could have an impact on you.

Typical locations

Accommodation should ideally be within walking distance of the main university buildings, but this is not always possible in cities, in which case good transport links to the campus or other sites are essential.

Students prefer to live near shops for groceries and areas close to the city centre are popular for the nightlife and part-time work, so good locations tend to be in city centres or busy suburbs, near stations and bus routes. Students also like living near fellow undergraduates, so opt for a road or area where there are already student properties rather than branching out somewhere new unless you are aiming at mature students.

What you need to provide

Students tend to be working to a tight budget and cannot afford high rents, so you need to maximise the number of rooms or beds for your property. Bedrooms can be quite small. Very few students will be willing to share a room unless they are a couple.

A real bonus is to be able to offer secure bike storage: many students cycle, bike theft is endemic and a bike stored in a communal hallway has a lot of nuisance value. Good security locks on windows and doors will also be a bonus as students are particularly vulnerable to theft. Broadband is essential, whereas items like en-suites and television packages are a bonus (see page 30).

In the kitchen of larger houses, several people may want to cook at the same time, so a microwave as well as a cooker is useful, as is a large fridge and plenty of storage space. Some landlords save expense by not fitting items such as washing machines or dishwashers, which can be hired by the tenant. Put in flooring that is easy to clean, robust or cheap to replace, such as tiling or vinyl.

With kitchens you can invest in a heavy-duty kitchen unit carcass, but then ensure that you get cheap doors and a cheap, easy to replace worktop. For showers, make sure you have one that is thermostatically controlled. You should also look for one with parts that can be replaced if they go wrong and are easy to access – you don't want to have to re-tile after a shower is fixed!

How to find tenants

- **University accommodation agencies.** Many educational establishments operate accreditation schemes listing landlords who fulfil certain criteria such as having current Gas Safe Registered (gas) and NICEIC, ECA or NAPIT (electrical) safety certificates and staff will often act as arbiter if disputes occur. Whether or not they run such a scheme, accommodation offices are a valuable route to finding tenants at little cost to you.
- **Advertising in the student newspaper/internet** and on noticeboards and cards in shop windows in areas frequented by students.
- **Word of mouth** is the best recommendation, and if you have a solid reputation and suitable accommodation, you should be able to find tenants quite easily unless the market becomes saturated.

Helpful advice

Students use the internet for research and leisure and your property is more attractive to them if it has a broadband connection because it is far faster. Overseas students, in particular, will value this facility. For those wishing to download music and videos, unlimited packages are best and you need wireless broadband. If you sign up for broadband, make a note of when the contract expires so that you can renew, if your tenants require it.

BE CAREFUL!

It is common to ask parents to act as guarantors for their child (see page 80). Get contact details for the parents because if there is a dispute, particularly over the tenant's behaviour, you can get them involved: they are likely to have more sway over their child than you have as a landlord.

Houses in Multiple Occupation (HMOs)

As a general guide, the definition of a house in multiple occupation (HMO) is that three unrelated people share a property's facilities. In April 2006, however, the Government introduced licensing for some types of properties that are classed as an HMO in England and Wales (see page 32 and pages 179–80 for details of these for Scotland and page 187 for Northern Ireland).

For advice on HMOs, see pages 30–3. Check with your local council or experienced letting agent if you need a licence and what adjustments you need to make to ensure your buy-to-let property is legal under the new rules. Go to Savills Research at www.savills.co.uk/research, which covers student accomodation in the UK.

These new licensing rules mean that a property that is on three or more habitable storeys (including attics or basements) and is occupied by five or more people (who are not all in the same family) who share some communal rooms is defined as an HMO that requires a licence.

While this is the general guideline, rules around HMOs and licensing are complex and you should contact a lettings' agency specialising in HMOs, or with your local authority, to find out whether or not you need a licence.

Since 2010, local authorities can impose their own 'additional licensing' and definition of a licensed HMO. Typical rules for a licensed HMO are:

- **A minimum room size** for one individual (6.5 square metres is a typical minimum).
- **Not allowing more than two people** to sleep in each room, including children.
- **Meeting stringent fire regulations,** such as smoke alarms, fire extinguishers, fire doors and fire blankets in all kitchen areas.
- **Having emergency lighting** in areas such as a hallway that would be used to escape fire or flood.
- **Upgrading floors and ceilings** to enhance sound proofing.

It's all in the detail

You may decide that female students are going to look after your property more carefully than males - or that it is more suited to men, or couples. Although you can't specify what gender your tenants can be, you can influence it subtly by, for example, taking the decoration into consideration to make it look more feminine, or setting up double rooms to encourage couples.

The tenant's take

As a student on a budget, price is crucial. You may be able to get better deals by teaming up with friends and renting together, and a group that intends to share accommodation can share the toil of finding it too.

Ask around: if you hear of a room being available before it hits the market, you might get first refusal, and the landlord will be pleased to get a tenant promptly. See page 113 for advice on choosing people to live with.

It is often cheaper to rent a room in a family home. You will benefit from a fairly high standard of accommodation. The downside is you won't be sharing with other students (for some this is an upside!) and you need to get on with the other people in the house (which might include children), who won't share your lifestyle.

Make sure you agree some rules about how you are going to get along together - see also page 113.

Fees for licensing vary widely from £300 to over £1,000, but local authorities are allowed to offer reductions to landlords on their accreditation schemes or to those who pay promptly. It is usually the landlord who is responsible for paying Council Tax on HMO premises.

Typical locations

Larger properties are usually found in the older parts of cities and apart from being located near the university or college, being near shops and parking spaces are handy.

What you need to provide

What you need to provide is similar to student accommodation. Bedrooms are likely to be larger than those you would consider suitable for a student. The kitchen must allow for several tenants to store and cook food, so a cooker, separate hob and a microwave will help. This room will be used a lot, so install units with good carcasses so you can just change the doors every few years. A hard-wearing work surface is important, too. The shower should be easy to repair (with working parts exposed rather than hidden behind tiles) and be thermostatically controlled and maintain water pressure when other water appliances are being used. Having en-suite bathrooms for some rooms will help, and, failing that, a sink in the room and a separate toilet helps reduce bathroom queues.

How to find tenants

- **Let to a group of people** who know each other. They can sign one contract – easier to administer.
- **Advertise for individual tenants** in local newspapers. You may get a better return letting but you will need to advertise more, do more paperwork and repeat the process every time one person moves out. Try also advertising on the noticeboards of large institutions, such as hospitals, companies and supermarkets.
- **Employ a letting agency.** More efficient, but you could be faced with fees for placing a succession of tenants.

Letting to LHA tenants

Social let housing is accommodation provided by councils, housing associations, charities or private landlords where the tenant's rent is fully or partly funded by a charity or, if renting privately from 7 April 2008, through the Local Housing

For more information on HMOs, visit **www.gov.uk**, **www.communities.gov.uk/publications/housing/licensinghouses**, **www.landlordzone.co.uk/HMOs1.htm** and **www.spareroom.co.uk**.

Allowance (LHA) and, from 2013, Universal Credit.

Letting to social tenants can be worthwhile, but you need to work closely with the local housing office and, if possible, become a local authority accredited landlord. You can check out likely rents by visiting www.gov.uk and searching for LHADirect.

Letting to social tenants can be harder than to privately funded ones, especially with the caps on Housing Benefit and the switch to Universal Credit from 2013. Not all lenders will offer you a mortgage in this sector, insurance is more expensive and tenants are mainly given their money to pay directly to you – which doesn't always happen. The upside, though, is that they tend to stay longer in the property if the building is well looked after, which means fewer voids and better cashflow. They may even undertake maintenance tasks, such as decorating, which could add value to your property.

The tenant's take

You can check if the property is licensed as an HMO by looking in the register of the local housing authority. Beware! HMOs are often the chosen route of rogue landlords who are more interested in taking your money than providing a decent roof over your head. To avoid rogue landlords:

- Ask which deposit protection scheme your deposit will be looked after by (see pages 83–4).
- Always ask for up-to-date gas and electrical safety certificates.
- If it's not a licensed HMO, ask to see the Energy Performance Certificate on the property.

If your prospective tenant is applying for Housing Benefit (Universal Credit from 2013), ask him or her to sign a letter giving permission for the relevant staff to talk to you about the application: then

Local Housing Allowance and Universal Credit

Local Housing Allowance (LHA) is paid to tenants on low incomes who moved into the private rented sector (PRS) after 1 April 2008. Housing Benefit is paid to people who are not in the PRS or haven't moved since this time. The payment is made directly to the tenant unless there are mitigating circumstances, including tenant rent arrears. If you have a tenant who needs help securing LHA, visit www.dwp.gov.uk to download the information and claim form (except for Northern Ireland). For new claimants from 2013, Housing Benefit will not exist, but the same support is expected to be applied to the Universal Credit. However, if someone is renting a three-bedroom property and they don't need three bedrooms, they may have their housing element cut.

you will know how it is progressing and whether (and when) the tenant is likely to be able to move in. You can ask for an interim payment if you allow the tenant to move in while the application is being processed.

What you need to provide

As the tenants often have children, they are likely to want a garden and at least two bedrooms. The property must be furnished to legal standards and decoration needs to be clean. Bedsits, studio flats and flats above shops are generally not accepted by housing associations.

How to find tenants

- **The local council.** Many councils keep a list of registered providers of social housing and will allocate tenants to properties. They may also run an accreditation scheme for private landlords.
- **Housing associations** usually own the properties they let out, but it is sometimes possible to lease property to a housing association or local authority for a specified period: they will then handle letting, rent collection and day-to-day running. Such schemes typically run for two-year stretches and have the particular benefit that the landlord's rental income is guaranteed for all of that period.
- **Charities.** Some charities secure rental accommodation from the private sector for the people they are supporting. They will usually engage a local letting agent to look after the property on their behalf, so speak to agents to see if they work with any charities you might like to help to support.

The tenant's take

Council housing departments allocate social housing in their district according to a points system or banding scheme, which assesses need. However, some councils offer choice-based letting's(CBL) schemes. This allows approved tenants regarded as a high priority to apply for specific properties that are advertised in the neighbourhood. You still need to apply for Housing Benefit or Local Housing Allowance (Universal Credit from 2013) well before your planned moving date as the process is not always fast. Be realistic: the benefit is designed to cover your needs, not necessarily your wants, so don't expect a three-bedroom property if you only need two. Stay within the terms of the benefit - you can't allow other people to live in the property and must inform the claims department if your income or living circumstances change.

For more information on social lets, see pages 150–6. For more information about CBL schemes, contact your local council and visit **http://england.shelter.org.uk**. To find places to rent, go to **www.councilexchangesite.co.uk** and **www.homesandcommunities.co.uk**.

Buying property to let

3

If you have already bought and sold property for yourself and your family, forget everything you did before! Buying property to let to someone else requires a business plan, an understanding of what income and capital growth your buy to let will deliver.

Researching the local market

It is important to have read the previous chapter to ensure that you make a decision on which is the best market to aim for before you buy a property to let out.

You also need a good grasp of the market in your target area:

- What types of let are required?
- Are there any gaps in the market? Why has no one else met them?
- Can you afford to purchase a property of the right type?
- How will you target the right tenants in this market?

Critical to the process is to understand how the market differs now and in the future. For example, if you buy in a city centre, what will the supply and demand be for the future? Are more people moving into the area or leaving it? Is it reliant on a few major employers who could up and leave? Are so many homes being built that capital growth and rental income will be held back? Ideally you want to invest in an area where supply is restricted and demand will grow for your target tenant market.

Background info

There are a number of very useful things that you can do to find out about the best market to let to in an area you are interested in.

Visit 'letting only' agents

These tend to be first port of call for anyone looking to let, so it is worth popping in, particularly during quieter times early in the week.

Ideally, start with a lettings specialist who is a member of the National Approved Lettings Scheme (NALs) or the Association of Residential Letting Agents (ARLA). Those that also sell property may be keener to sell to you. A good lettings only agent will be happy to brief you on the market as they will only want you to buy properties they can let easily – especially if they don't earn money from selling property.

Questions to ask a lettings specialist include:

- **What types of properties** are easy to let?
- **Are there any types of let** that are short in availability locally?
- **What is the variation in rent** for the different types of let?
- **Are there any types of let** that have noticeably long or short periods of being empty?
- **Where are the best areas** to look for property to suit the different target letting markets?

Summary of the key differences when buying a property to let		
Buying process	**Buying a property for you**	**Buying a property to let**
Looking for property	■ Choose the best location you can afford	■ Choose a location that gives you the highest yield (return) or captial growth (see page 43)
Choosing a property	■ Find a property that suits your own requirements, needs and wants	■ Choose a property that suits the needs and wants of the market you have chosen to let to
Financing a property	■ Gain the best rate from a lender ■ Put down the highest deposit that you are able to	■ Will often need a specific buy-to-let mortgage ■ Will have to put down a minimum deposit, but don't always put down the highest deposit you can
The legals of buying a property	■ Look for information that affects how you live in the property	■ Look for information that affects how or if you can let it out legally
Surveying a property	■ Currently a survey is optional, although you should always have the minimum of a HomeBuyer Report	■ A survey not just of the structure, but of the gas and electrics, too. Safety is essential as you may be liable for any damage the property may inflict on tenants. You will also require an energy performance certificate (EPC) to understand how the EPC affects rental potential
Preparing a property	■ Choose décor, fixtures and fittings to suit your taste and lifestyle	■ Choose décor, fixture and fittings that will stand the test of tenants and suit the lifestyle you are aiming to let to. If renting as an HMO, check with an experienced letting agent and local council that it meets legal requirements
Furnishing a property	■ As above, you would choose furnishings that would suit your lifestyle	■ Choose whether you are going to offer furnishings or not, and if you do, make sure they adhere to the regulations (see pages 74–5)
Repairing a property	■ Repair as soon as you can and to the standard that you want	■ Repair to legal requirements to match national and local regulations
Household bills	■ Choose which utilities you would want	■ Choose the best deals for tenants, consider energy saving measures

If a couple or more agents give you the same information, then you can be fairly sure that it is accurate. You can also 'watch the market' to help verify the information you have received about letting potential.

Watch the market

Unlike the buying and selling market, watching the letting market is a little more difficult as the process of putting a property up for let and then letting it can happen in less than 24 hours. However, it is an important part of researching what sort of let you will go for. The best way is to track a few properties of each type, checking how long it takes for them to be let. Look through the paper, or ask letting/estate agents. To help choose between different types of let, use the table, below.

You might find that the same types of let vary in how long it takes to let them and this type of research helps you to find out why. For example, it might be that the letting price is much higher, or that people prefer a top-floor flat, rather than a ground-floor flat, or indeed that one has parking and the other doesn't. All of these aspects are important to understand so that you can work out what property specifications you need to look for when going out to buy.

Small is big

The majority of rented properties have only one to three bedrooms. More people are living on their own than ever before, or as single parent families. In general:

- Studio and one-bedroom flats are less popular than two-bedroom flats.
- Smaller properties are typically cheaper. If you have a lot of money to invest, consider buying two or three small, two-bedroom properties rather than a large property that could prove much harder to rent to a more limited market unless you are considering HMOs (see pages 31–2).

Examples of different times it might take to let a property

Property	Date on market	Rental price per week	Date let	Time on market
Company let to a professional	1 September	£150	15 September	15 days
Student let (per room)	1 September	£85	10 September	10 days
Private professional let	1 September	£125	5 September	5 days
Social let	1 September	£80	2 September	2 days

Check on local authority research

This is a great resource for anyone looking to buy to let as a local authority plan gives you information, such as population trends, for example, are people moving into the area, maybe for temporary jobs? Perhaps there is growth in a young or old population that creates a need for smaller properties near shops, hospitals and public transport.

Looking at the local plan and housing need information can also give you an indication of what is happening to local transport. For example, there may be a new bus route, or train/tram terminal being built, or indeed a new road network that would speed up someone's journey to work and back. This could mean an increase in the potential population and therefore an increase in demand for properties to let.

Talk to local landlord groups and associations

These organisations may well be able to help. Although in theory you are 'in competition' with everyone, there are usually people who are willing to help and give you advice. Some may have been caught out on particular types of properties and may be happy for you to learn from their mistakes. However, always verify any advice you gain from people you don't know.

Approach other relevant organisations

If you are looking to research a particular type of let, such as company, student or social let, you could approach the local organisations that are likely to help the tenants find accommodation in the first place. For example, if you are looking at the market for company lets, then talk to some of the major organisations in the area – try their human resources, personnel or accommodation departments, if they have one.

For students (or indeed academics, who tend to move fairly frequently), talk to the local university or college accommodation department. The department will be able to tell you if you are better off finding a property to let to undergraduates, mature students or, better still, one of the visiting lecturers or professors.

If you are considering a social let, then chat to your local housing authority. Many run accreditation schemes, which are well worth joining. You should try your local housing association, too, as they are likely to know what is required in the area and what type of rent you could expect in return.

Local plans are available online through the website of your local council. To Find your local authority housing contacts, visit your local authority website or local council office, or look in your local phone book.

Finding the perfect location

The next step to buying a property is to establish what are the letting growth areas now and in the future. For example, you might find there is a shortage of student rents, but in two years' time this will reduce due to a planned development.

The internet

Unlike with buying and selling property, the internet does not help you research huge amounts of information about the letting market because it is fast moving and the information available tends to be out of date. It is useful, however, for finding average rental values in the markets you are interested in. There are various sites that concentrate on certain types of let (see below), which will help you find what is already available in your chosen area, and suggest areas to start looking.

For example, in Reading, Berkshire, there are known areas for student lets. These are typically the older, Victorian-style houses on the west side of the town. The rents in this region tend to be cheaper than the north, south or east and it's easy to get to college/university and the town centre – both major benefits to the student community!

If, however, you want to target the professional in Reading, then you are more likely to be looking at apartments around the centre, which make it easy to get to the large companies that are located in the town centre.

On the other hand, if you are looking more at letting out to families, then you are likely to need to target two- to three-bedroom houses, in good condition, with a garden, away from a main road and within easy reach of schools and local transport. An area that fits this description well is Lower Earley, just southeast of Reading, near Winnersh Triangle, a big area for offices and industrial companies. This example shows the value of local knowledge in deciding what sector of the required market to aim for.

A useful website to look at when considering different areas in which to buy is **www.zoopla.co.uk** and for renting rooms, go to: **www.spareroom.co.uk/rentalindex** and **uk.easyroommate.com/RC/flatshareindex/map**.

In newspapers

Another good place to look is the local property paper, *Loot* or *Daltons Weekly*. This will give you an idea of postcode areas to concentrate on for different types of let. Usually properties are listed by area and price, so some areas are quoted in 'price per week' and could be anything from £100 to over £500 a week, depending on the type of property, its location and who it is aimed at.

This research will also help you later on when you are looking for tenants/letting agents to help let your chosen property (see pages 66–73) as you will begin to get an idea of which agent or advertising route is likely to be the one to work with to reach your target market.

Local letting agents

As with who to look for, when researching the market, it is worth getting the 'lists' that the local agents produce on a weekly and sometimes daily basis to get an idea of where properties are for different markets. These lists are helpful as they:

- **Tend to be given** in price order.
- **Often have the date** the property becomes available to let – allowing you to gain some idea of how far in advance you may need to start marketing the property to gain a tenant.
- **Give an indication** of the prices you gain for each of the different postcodes.
- **Allow you to research the prices** that the properties available to let have sold for.

Letting agents (especially those that only let) can also assess property opportunities for you and may have ready made buy to let properties that other landlords want to sell. If they know the area really well, call them with the postcode of a property you are interested in and they should be able to give an indication of what its rental value might be worth and whether it is the right investment for you.

Local authority websites

These are extremely useful in identifying local areas that are likely to change. The changes to search for are:

- What regeneration and transport changes are there that might enhance an area's desirability?
- What new properties are being built and where, which might increase or decrease the value of future properties?

To find local papers in an area, go to the website **www.newspapersoc.org.uk** (the Newspaper Society) where you can search for daily and weekly local papers both paid for and free. Try also **www.loot.com**, the online version of Loot, and **www.daltonsproperty.com**.

Value versus rental income

Assessing a property based on its financial return as opposed to whether you think it is a nice home or not is the biggest difference between buying to let and buying a property for yourself.

When buying, you are likely to have salary constraints and be limited by how much of a deposit you can afford. When buying to let, there are far more important things that the lender will want to know before they will be happy to lend on a property for you to let.

The return on letting

Think of buying to let as running a business. You basically need to make sure that your turnover (that is, your rent) is in excess of the costs of buying/funding and maintaining the property. As a guide, look for a property where the rent will exceed your running costs of the property by 20–30 per cent.

For an example, see the box below left. In this case, the profit means that the rent (that is, the income) is 20 per cent more than the costs, which is likely to cover the landlord for times when the property is not rented out, any large investment such as a broken boiler, and any tax he or she may have to pay on the rental income. It also gives an opportunity to reduce the rent should prices drop locally, and all without causing financial trouble that could mean having to sell the property.

Establishing the profit

Income	
Rent:	£600 per month
Costs	
Mortgage cost	£425 per month
Insurance	£15 per month
Maintenance	£50 per month
Household bills	£10 per month
Total costs:	**£500 per month**
Monthly gross profit therefore = £600 - £500 = £100	

Jargon buster

Rental yield The annual rent of a property as a percentage of its capital value or acquisition price.
Return on investment A more detailed analysis of income versus expenditure to establish a long-term view of earnings on a let property.
Turnover The amount you earn from rent.

Rental yield and return on investment

If you are going to make it as a property entrepreneur through letting property, terms such as **rental yield** and **return on investment** will become part of your daily vocabulary. They are no different to any term used in business to assess how profitable a venture is, and are used by companies to sell you property to let out and by letting agents to help you work out what is a good investment of your money – or not.

They are a good way to assess which type of rent and which type of property to purchase to help you make the most of your money. Don't forget there are lots of ways of making money and buying property to let can be a high risk strategy if you borrow too much. As you are investing for a return, you must compare returns to other investment methods, such as shares or a pension scheme.

Rental yield

This is calculated from everything that you spend on buying a property, from expenses such as petrol to drive around and look for property to the cost of any money that you borrow to fund the let, and then takes into consideration the amount of money you earn over and above the costs/ investment. As a guide, the table on page 44 shows some of the costs that you need to consider.

The simplest way to establish your rental yield is to subtract running costs from the amount of rent earned and divide that figure by how much the property cost. Multiply your answer by 100, to express your rental yield as a percentage (see opposite for an example and also the table on page 45). This allows you to compare different investment decisions. There are many different ways that yield and return on investment are measured.

Return on investment

As an example of how to work this slightly more complicated calculation, see the table on page 45. By working out some sample calculations, you will help yourself to choose which type of property you want to let out.

Usually houses in multiple occupation yield higher returns as you rent each room rather than a whole house. You have to spend more to legally let them though.

On the other hand, better-paying company lets can be somewhat volatile, depending on the economy. You may also face higher levels of competition, which will result in your property to lie empty or get lower returns from decreasing rent in order to compete.

For help assessing rental yields and return on investment, visit **www.propertychecklists.co.uk** and **www.paragon-mortgages.co.uk**, and for affordability calculators also go to the Paragon website.

Costs to consider when establishing your rental yield

One-off costs of buying

Research costs

Subscriptions to websites

Books that you purchase to research the let

Any professional fees incurred

Costs of finding a property

Petrol/travel costs

Food out on full days

Overnight stays

Cost of financing the property

Mortgage fees (administration, arrangement and broker fees)

Deposit monies

Cost of buying the property

Survey

Legal fees

Stamp duty land tax

Any removals fees

Gas/electricity safety checks

'Use these lists as the basis for working out your potential rental yield. Make sure you include all your costs.'

Ongoing costs

Costs of preparing/keeping the property ready for rent

New carpets/curtains/ kitchen/bathroom

Maintenance, for example, painting or fixing the roof

Any appliances

Gas/electricity safety checks

Finance costs

Mortgage interest/repayment costs

Buildings/contents insurance

Professional insurance/ protecting your let

Letting costs

Finding a tenant

Contracts

Letting agent fees

Inventory costs

Energy performance certificate (see page 54)

Deposit protection fee, which may be included in your letting fee (see pages 83-6)

Optional extra cost of becoming a member of one of the landlord associations (see pages 67 and 103)

Exit fees (when you sell the property)

Estate agent fees

Energy Performance Certificate

Legal fees

Removal fees

Examples of establishing the return on your investment

There are lots of methods to calculate yield and return on your investment. Here is one example, worked out before tax, that helps to compare different buy-to-let opportunities.

	Student let	Company let
Property purchase	£120,000	£250,000
Costs of buying	£2,500	£10,000
Home improvement	£0	£ 5,000
Total investment:	£122,500	£265,000
Expected monthly rent	£775	£1,750
Annual rental income	£9,300	£21,000
Likely amount of time empty (voids)	15%	10%
Annual rental income after voids	£7,905	£18,900
Deduct expected annual expenses	£1,080	£3,000
Income after expenses and voids	£6,825	£15,900
Gross income yield per annum◆	5.57%	6%
Mortgage loan	£90,000	£175,000
Annual mortgage costs▲	£5,400	£10,500
Annual income (after expenses and voids less mortgage costs)	£1,425	£5,400
Initial investment for purchase (capital investment)●	£32,500	£90,000
Net income yield per annum■	4.38%	6%
Capital growth after 5 years:		
Estimate future property value at 3%	£139,100	£290,000
Deduct outstanding mortgage	£90,000	£175,000
Deduct selling costs	£3,300	£6,800
Future value of investment	£45,800	£108,200
Growth of initial investment	£13,300	£18,200
Capital return on investment	8.18% per annum	4.04% per annum (RoI)✦

◆ Gross income yield = Income after expenses and voids ÷ property value x 100

▲ An annual mortgage cost is that of financing the loan and you will have to get this from a buy-to-let mortgage calculator

● The initial investment = purchase price + costs of buying – mortgage loan

■ Net income yield = income after expenses and voids – mortgage costs ÷ initial investment x 100

✦ RoI = Growth of initial investment/initial investment x 100/number of years (in this case, five)

Financing your buy to let

Approach financing a property as if you were funding a new business. Be aware, too, that gaining a mortgage for a buy to let is different to gaining one for your own home. There are two types of financing to consider.

Letting a property you have lived in

If you are already living in a property and are moving out, the first thing you need to do is to inform your lender and let them know you are planning to let your property to tenants.

Depending on the reason why – for example, company relocation, moving abroad – your lender may let you continue with your current mortgage or request that you move to a buy-to-let mortgage instead, or just charge a slightly higher interest rate. It is important to check out alternative offers from other companies at this point as they may well be more competitive than your own lender.

They will be likely to want to assess your property for rental value to ensure that it meets their lending criteria as a property being let rather than lived in.

Buying a property specifically to let

For most buy to lets, the mortgage company will require that the gross rent you receive from letting the property is 125–130 per cent of the mortgage costs you will incur before they will consider lending to you.

Differences between mortgage for your home and buying to let

Mortgage	Buying for yourself	Buying to let
Deposit	Require 10%+	Usually 25–40% required
How much you can borrow	Earnings related	Related to your financial security and the rental income versus costs
Survey	Requires value of the property	Requires a value of the property, plus independent verification of the rental income
Fees	Tend to be fairly competitive	May pay more as a business venture and interest can be off-set against income

The lender will also assess the value of the property, and whatever their valuation (which may be lower than what you are offering to pay for the property), they will then offer you 60–75 per cent of that value. This leaves you to put down the rest of the money in the form of a deposit.

Over and above the rental income and the property value, the lender will also take into consideration your income to check that you can afford the property should there be a downturn in the lettings market.

If you already have some properties you are letting out, the lender is likely to check your current borrowing versus current rental income. If you are too much of a risk – for example, if your gearing is above 75 per cent – they are less likely to lend.

> **Jargon buster**
>
> **Gearing** How much you borrow as a proportion of an independent valuation of the property/property portfolio.

The credit crunch

This has caused lenders to offer money more cautiously with a view that property prices might fall or buyers might default. As a result, flexible lending for buy-to-let investors, which was outside the normal 85 per cent lending, has stopped and on new build flats, some lenders have reduced their loan-to-value lending to 60 per cent. Anyone with a history of bad debts, however small, may not be able to secure money. The second effect is the cost of the mortgage. Initially lenders increased the cost of buy-to-let mortgages, but as they have proved successful for lenders, so costs and mortgage rates have become more competitive.

On the other hand, some lenders have restricted the number of properties for which they will provide mortages to any one person. More now than ever, you need to source a good mortgage deal by consulting IFAs mortgage brokers and lenders directly.

> **Lenders' fees**
>
> The types of charges you are likely to pay will vary by lender, but will tend to run to several thousand pounds. Some lenders charge a fixed fee while others charge a percentage of the mortgage value. You will also need to fork out a valuation fee, which could be anything from £200.

For more information on buying a property, see the Which? Essential Guide: *Buy, Sell & Move House*.

What to look for in a property

Although there are different things that you would look out for to meet the needs of specific types of let (see pages 22–34), there are many things that you should check for, whatever type of property let you are thinking about.

Specific property lets

If you are looking for a property to let, bear in mind the likely individual requirements of the type of rental market you are going to aim your property to – see the table, opposite.

Unless you are planning to renovate a property to let, check you are purchasing a structurally sound property before you make an offer. So if you are viewing properties, follow the checklists on pages 50–2 and then ensure you have the correct surveys so you know you have purchased a sound investment, rather than one that eats up any profit you may make.

The surveys you need to have done include a surveyor, gas engineer and electrician, but a good look around a property can save you thousands of pounds of wasted money on making an offer for a property you can't legally let and have to pull out of. Alternatively, it might mean you can make a lower offer to cover the cost of updating it to legal standards.

A few tips on location

The truism that location is crucial when choosing property is just as applicable when buying to let for your chosen market:

- Tenants may not have cars, so local transport links are essential.
- Concentrate on streets that are popular to live on and have shops nearby.
- View at different times of day to check on traffic conditions and noise levels.
- Upmarket company lets often go to managers on secondment from abroad who will have families, so a location near an international school is a big bonus.
- Buying property near where you live allows you to draw on your knowledge of the area and be on hand to deal with problems. However, it is more important to identify where the properties that serve your chosen market and give the best yield are located.

Choosing a property to match your let of choice

Type of Let	Number of bedrooms	Internal décor	Furnishings	Parking space	Garden
Student	3+	■ Blank canvas, easy to re-decorate between tenancies	■ Meeting legal and safety requirements, but cheap and easy to replace	■ One or two ideal, but not a necessity	■ Ideal if more than three people renting
Social	2+	■ Welcoming but easy to decorate	■ Meeting legal and safety requirements, but cheap and easy to replace ■ May have own furniture to bring	■ One ideally	■ Yes if renting to a family with children
Company	1+	■ Follows current trends, chic	■ Up to date and good quality, such as leather sofas	■ Two, ideally secured	■ Not required
Young professional	1+	■ Follows current trends, or blank canvas	■ Mid range quality, but follows current fashion, may want to furnish themselves	■ At least one, ideally two	■ Some will require a garden, especially with an eating out area, others not interested
Family	2+	■ Blank canvas, easy to maintain and decorate after tenants have left	■ Likely to have own furnishings, otherwise easy to clean such as imitation leather	■ At least one	■ Yes, grassed for children to play in

Viewing checklist

Roof and chimney

Look at these from the front, back and side of the property (if possible). The key things to look out for are any obviously missing tiles or parts of the roof; ensuring that the chimneys are straight; and that there are no cracks or heavy wear and tear on the bricks.

If you don't, this could end up in the roof/chimney leaking over time, rotting the timbers underneath and causing thousands of pounds worth of damage. It is also a very good idea to go up into the loft and check that the roof felt is intact and there is the recommended level of required insulation (290mm thick). Look for any holes that might show light, any decay on the timbers suggesting an infestation of some kind and any leaks – usually shown by stains or wet/damp patches.

Flat roofs are a must to check out. Take a ladder and look at any flat roofs as the life of these range from a few years to 15 years plus. Knowing how sound a flat roof can be could save you thousands of pounds in fixing one.

Case study Nadine

On one property, Nadine's survey showed up damp in the front room. The surveyor looked outside only to find that around the bay window, the previous owner had dug a hole below ground level, filled it with concrete at the bottom and then built a brick wall around the window bay. This was effectively creating a well when it rained as the water coming down had nowhere to drain to! Nadine fixed the problem by having the concrete at the bottom taken out and replaced with gravel, allowing the water to drain away and the wall to dry – and all for a few hundred pounds investment. This piece of creative thinking avoided thousands of pounds of re-plastering and damp proofing at a later date as it was caught early enough.

Viewing during or just after a bout of rain is ideal for these checks, so don't be put off viewing properties during an inconvenient storm: it could turn out to be a real blessing.

How much to maintain and upgrade?

If you plan to own your buy-to-let property for the standard 15–20 years, it is essential to confirm the replacement timings and costs for everything. For example, during your ownership do you have to replace the roof? How much will it cost? Will the windows need upgrading? How green is the property? What will you need to spend to ensure the property is energy efficient so you can legally let it in the future?

Guttering and drainage

This is as important as the roof structure as poor guttering and drainage can cause horrendous damage to a home, resulting in the worst cases in subsidence of the property – which is very expensive to fix. The key here is to catch the property when it is wet and check that all the joints are healthy, with no bits of guttering 'hanging down' or not properly linked to the next piece.

Check, too, where all the water drains out. It should go into proper drains, and the area around the drains (such as nearby walls) should not be unduly soaking wet.

Concrete around a house can cause the build-up of water and therefore damp in the walls – especially when the property is on a slope. So if you see any concrete around the walls, find out from the surveyor if it is likely to cause any problems, and cost out having the concrete taken away and replacing it with gravel, which allows water to soak away.

External walls

Check for cracks in a property. Most are likely to turn out to be harmless and on older properties they tend to exist as land has settled over time or, indeed, on new properties, they form a few years after a property has been built and there is some settlement onto the land. The main cracks to worry about are large ones with no obvious cause. For example, cracks below a window may mean that solid wooden windows were taken out and replaced with plastic ones without adding a lintel to hold the weight of the bricks. At worst, it could mean subsidence. This can be caused by damp, or by movement below the house, which is more serious and would need costly investigation.

Some external rendering has a minimum life, such as 25 years. Some of these coverings can damage a property by not allowing the walls to 'breathe', so letting out the moisture created inside the property. Some renders provide additional protection to the property, but if cracks appear, check what damage this is causing as rain may be able to get in, creating further problems, such as introducing damp, or freezing and expanding, which will enlarge the crack.

Ask your surveyor to comment on this type of covering if you have it on the property you are considering buying to let.

Windows and doors

There are two key issues here: maintenance and security. A

For a free viewing checklist that you can download, go to **www.which.co.uk/viewing-checklist**.

rented property needs to be low maintenance, as making repairs can be expensive, disrupt life for the tenant and could even require the property to be vacated. In particular, what you don't want is wooden windows that are rotting and require lots of attention, particularly if they are of a 'non-standard' size as they will have to be made specially and be repainted every two years. Security is often an important issue for tenants, so good security locks on windows and five-lever, two-bolt mortice locks are an asset. The ideal property for rent has easy-to-maintain UPVC windows and doors offering excellent security.

Internally

As a landlord, look for a property that seems to require minimum investment in terms of time and money. You want easy-to-maintain floors, such as those covered with laminate (as long as it is not a flat), stone or vinyl rather than carpets, which can stain easily, require regular cleaning and will probably need to be replaced every 2–3 years.

Walls are easier to maintain when painted rather than wallpapered, and look for areas of condensation or damp, particularly in the kitchen and bathroom or an en suite, as this can be expensive to sort out too.

In the kitchen and bathroom, there is often a choice between having long-lasting items that you invest in and hope the tenant appreciates and looks after or a cheap but 'stylish' kitchen, which can be replaced every 2–3 years, giving the property a 'fresh' appeal and helping to let it more regularly. It is relatively easy and cheap to replace cupboard doors, which is a good option every few years, provided the basic carcass is of good quality. Check how smoothly the drawers open and how sturdy the carcasses are.

Tenants will want at least a shower – and a clean one at that – and ideally a bath with a shower above. If more than two people will be occupying the property, you need washing facilities for more than one person at a time: no one likes to queue for the shower!

What to look for, what to ignore

Look at any potential letting property you are considering with a tenant's eyes. Tenants are most attracted to properties that are clean, easy to maintain, offering plenty of space for the money, and in a convenient location. Try not to be put off if your reaction is, 'Wow, the wallpaper is horrible!' Although grim décor can make a property look terrible, it is easy to correct with a pot of white paint. You can transform the look of a room quickly and cheaply by re-decorating. Badly decorated properties can be bargains because buyers are often put off.

Other checks

A frightening number of people still do not have a proper, independent survey carried out on a property before they buy. Even if you follow the viewing advice on pages 50–2, that does not mean you have checked everything you need. An independent surveyor will:

- Check the condition of the structure of the property.
- Check the condition of the internal walls and floors where they can be accessed.
- Advise on immediate, short-term and long-term repairs that the property needs.

This will give you a good idea of the likely maintenance costs of the property. If they are more than you expected, then you could use this to negotiate down the value of the property – hence reducing your costs and increasing the potential of your financial return.

It is important to ensure that you have a minimum of a HomeBuyer Report or a building survey if the property is pre-World War Two or in a poor state of repair or of an unusual construction. Or if you have a new build, make sure it's in top condition with a snagging survey. This gives you some protection should things go wrong that the surveyor hasn't picked up, or indeed show that the property has too much wrong with it to bring it up to letting standards.

The costs vary across the country for surveys and are between £300 and £1,000. You can deduct the cost from your income, so it is 'tax deductible' (see pages 116–17).

However, the survey that is done on the property is not the only one you will need when you buy looking to let. It is also crucial that you check the gas and electrics, drainage, energy efficiency and any appliances that the vendor is leaving behind.

Gas and electric survey

As Energy Performance Certificates are now supplied with a property for sale, you will gain some information about the property's electrics and/or gas. This will include the likely costs of gas and electricity bills and how energy efficient the property is.

However, it is essential as a potential future landlord of the property you are buying, that you have various surveys done to ensure it can be let legally and, from a landlord's perspective, in as stress-free a way as possible. These surveys include the plumbing system, gas installation and appliances, central heating and electrical installation.

The surveys report on the condition of the items above that are easy to access and say if they need to be replaced or are within the law. Without this, no agent or tenant should accept to let or rent your property. The exception is for people who are renting out a room in their own property when you may not have to have the gas and electric safety certificate as it is your own home. However, anyone buying a property or looking to rent out to others should really have this survey

BE CAREFUL!

When letting a property, the landlord is liable to the tenant(s) for anything that goes wrong with the gas and electrics and to legally let a property, you must protect yourself by having safety certificates.

done too, for yourself as much as your potential new tenant.

There are several companies that have been created especially to help with this type of survey. The charges are not cheap, and vary according to the size of the company. They range from £150 upwards. However, it is a legal requirement for the gas to be safe and all costs are tax deductible (see page 116).

Alternatively, a qualified electrician and Gas Safety Registered engineer will be able to check the property and give you the certificates, or advise on how much it will cost to bring the property up to legal letting standards.

Tenants in common or joint tenants?

When you buy a home with a spouse or partner, you usually buy it as 'joint tenants'. If you are buying a property for investment purposes, consider buying as 'tenants in common' as it can be more tax efficient and you can decide who your part ownership of a home can be left to in your will.

Legal checks

When buying a property to let, make sure that you understand exactly what you are buying and what costs you are liable for. This is particularly relevant if you are purchasing a flat and/or leasehold property. If you are unsure of any legal clause, ask a solicitor to advise you. Here are some legal phrases to look out for.

Rights of way

This is simply what right people may have to walk across your

Energy performance certificates (EPCs)

Every property has to be sold with an Energy Performance Certificate and let with one when a tenant views a property. EPCs also include an estimate of the size of the property, which can be useful when comparing properties.

As a landlord, ideally you want a property with a high rating or one that is easy to increase the energy efficiency. If you have a good EPC rating (within A to C), this should appeal to prospective tenants as it means lower heating bills. New builds should have an A rating and the worst properties will be those with no loft insulation, double glazing or cavity walls.

An EPC costs from £50 and you can organise your EPC by choosing an energy assessor from www.epcregister.com or your letting agent should be able to do this for you. When buying, check that you can use the EPC from the vendor.

Useful websites for the gas and electrics survey are **www.gassaferegister.co.uk**, **www.competentperson.co.uk** and **www.niceic.org.uk**. For more information about EPCs, go to **www.gov.uk** and search for 'EPC'.

garden, or how costs are shared for a jointly accessed driveway or area where the rubbish bins are kept. If you are buying to let, you want as few problems as possible with the neighbours as disputes are much harder to resolve if you are not on the spot. So make sure that you are clear about what the rights of way are and build into any contract with the tenant that they respect these.

Restrictions of use or change of use

This is particularly relevant when buying to let as there may be something in the contract that suggests you cannot turn a house you are planning to buy into two flats to let out. It may be that you plan to have an office in part of the property and let the rest. Check that there are no restrictions of this kind with your legal company.

Covenants

Some properties are sold with a covenant attached. For example, a property with a large garden that looks ripe for development may have a covenant that stops anyone from building on the land unless they pay a premium to a previous owner, or maybe you just aren't allowed to build anything else or even extend the building until the end of the covenant.

Property boundaries

It is important, too, to check where your property starts and finishes

Case study Mr Grabel

Mr Grabel wanted to start buying flats to let out in a small town near the sea on the south coast. He went to an auction to see how much properties were and happened to see a property that seemed really cheap and in a good location. It should have struck Mr Grabel that caution was a good idea at this point, but instead he went ahead, started bidding and then secured the property.

Unfortunately, as Mr Grabel had bought at auction, he was committed to completing on the flat within 28 days. This was despite the fact that he hadn't checked the property's condition or, more importantly, the legal expenses associated with owning the flat, and as it was a flat, that meant the lease.

Once bought, Mr Grabel went into the flat and found it in quite good condition and indeed in a good location. He went about spending money smartening up the flat, with fresh paint, new carpets, a new kitchen and even a new shower. At this point, he then sat down to read the lease agreement. What a shock!

Mr Grabel found a clause that prevented any owners of the flats renting out the property to a tenant.

The result was that Mr Grabel then had to put the property back on the market, for not much more money, and lose a substantial amount of money as well as time in the process. The purchasing costs would have included the legal advice and stamp duty land tax and then on top of this there were the selling fees via an estate agent and yet more legal advice.

All in all, this turned out to be a very expensive mistake for Mr Grabel, which he could easily have avoided!

and exactly what you are buying. You don't want a boundary dispute while you are trying to rent out the property and need to be clear as to what to put in the contract with the tenant to ensure they understand what they are renting and what belongs to the neighbours.

Leasehold properties

It is essential that you check the rules and regulations within the leasehold, particularly in a leasehold flat, as some do not allow you to sublet a room, or the property itself. Many people have made this mistake, not read the agreement in detail and then found that after to purchasing they can't then let out the property.

You must also ensure that the legal company/letting agent that prepares the contract with your tenant incorporates any 'noise' and 'communal use' into it.

The lease agreement will also lay out the costs of **ground rent** and **service charges** and it is important that you understand how these are worked out and what you are liable for. For example, it may be that the whole block needs new water tanks or windows and your share of this cost is £5,000. This could be a nasty shock if you didn't realise you were liable.

It is also important to establish how any repairs (together with the service charge and ground rent) are paid for – by you or the tenant. Bear in mind that no tenant is likely to sign up for a 6–12-month contract if they know they will have to fork out £5,000 for repairs on a building they do not own even part of!

Lender restrictions

Your lender may impose some restrictions on you and how you run your lettings business and your legal representative needs to ensure that you are aware of all of these before making the purchase. For example, some lenders will insist that you let only on an 'assured shorthold tenancy' basis (see pages 128–32), and many lenders will not lend on properties that are intended to be let to social tenants, which is important if this is the market you have chosen to target.

Jargon buster

Ground rent Payment by the leaseholder to the freeholder. Low sums are sometimes referred to as a peppercorn rent.

Leasehold Ownership for a set period, most commonly applied to flats and other shared buildings.

Service charges Payment for maintenance of shared areas, such as communal hallways, the roof and drains.

See pages 125–6 for more information on running a letting business, on both asmall- and large-scale basis. See also **www.holidayletmortgages.co.uk/** for specialist lettings finance.

Buying property already let

One way of buying a property and ensuring instant income is to buy one that is already let. This will need an assured shorthold tenancy agreement and you will have to find a lender that is prepared to lend under these circumstances.

If you are buying with a sitting tenant, make sure the legal company you use to make the purchase has plenty of experience in this field: even if it costs you slightly more, this is definitely not a time to 'save money' when buying – it could cost you a fortune later on if you don't use the right person.

Finding a property to purchase

Most properties that are already let and are up for sale are sold via auction houses or directly from one investor to another. The auction house will typically advertise the property in its catalogue with these details:

- Guide price for the property (remember this means it may sell for less or much more).
- Number of tenants in the property.
- Rental income generated.
- Annual yield/return.

You can also talk to local estate agents and check local property papers to see if anyone is advertising a property for sale with tenants. Talk to local letting agents, too, and ask them if they know of any landlords who are likely to want to sell their property and investigate purchasing prior to it being put on the market.

What to look for

Unlike when you are buying property for yourself or buying a property to let out, there are many more things that you need to investigate – preferably before you make an offer.

Why is the landlord selling?

It may be for good reasons in that they just want to cash in on the capital growth of the property, or are moving abroad and want to sell off all their UK investments. However, there may be hidden factors, for example, the property is in desperate need of repairs or the tenants are complaining about things not working, or are not paying! Worse still, the landlord may be about to go bankrupt.

Alternatively, perhaps the landlord is getting daily complaints from unhappy neighbours – so make sure you pop by and ask the neighbours how they get on with the tenants before making an offer.

What is the general condition of the property?

Again, it might be that someone just hasn't the money, time or inclination to keep maintaining the property in good condition. They may not want the hassle of sourcing new boilers, bathrooms and kitchens and if these all need replacing, you need to be aware of the costs involved. It may be the case that the repairs are severe enough for the tenants to have to move out for a while and you will need to work out what happens if they do. Do you offer reduced rent or are they really happy to stay/move out to friends knowing that they will benefit from the upgrade?

Contracts with the tenants

This is the crux of whether the purchase is a sound investment or not. Basically, the agreements that you take over with incumbent tenants will determine:

- What your rights are as a landlord.
- What their rights as tenants are.
- What likely running/on-going costs you may have.
- Whether you can purchase the property and the tenants 'as a going concern'.

As far as the agreements are concerned, you will need to gain a copy of the first AND current tenancy agreements. Your legal representative may ask for these anyway, but the sooner you can read them – preferably before you make an offer and incur any expense – then the faster the purchase process will be too. You should also establish:

- The date the tenant first moved in.
- The payment record of the tenant(s).
- What level of deposit the landlord has taken and that this is transferable.
- If there are any possession notices that have been served.
- If there are any Section 21 notices (see page 163) as this is what the current landlord would send to advise a tenant that their agreement is coming to an end.

Jargon buster

Assured shorthold tenancy A form of tenancy that assures the landlord has a right to repossess the property at the end of the term specified in the tenancy agreement, which can be for any length of time.
Ordinary assured tenancy (also shortened to 'assured tenancy') A form of tenancy introduced where a property is let out as a separate dwelling and used as the tenant's only or main home. The tenant can stay in occupation until either he or she decides to leave or the landlord obtains a possession order.

Case study Mrs Elmer

Mrs Elmer decided that she wanted to expand her property portfolio. She was an experienced buy-to-let investor and was used to dealing with the legal aspects, money and the tenants. However, she had seen that some properties she would quite like to add to her portfolio were already let. She investigated buying a property with sitting tenants and found that if she could ensure there was an assured shorthold tenancy in place at the time of exchange, then finding finance would not be too difficult. On the other hand, buying a property with assured tenancy agreements could be much cheaper, but lending would be harder, or more expensive to obtain.

After going to estate agents and looking in the newspaper, the auction houses seemed to be the best bet. Before every auction, Mrs Elmer purchased the catalogue well in advance of the auction and then did a drive-by visit of the ones that she was interested in. Once she'd found several properties she liked, Mrs Elmer checked with one of the mortgage lenders that they would be happy to lend on a tenanted property.

For each property, she found out why the landlord was selling, spoke to neighbours to ask about the tenants and obtained a copy of the latest agreement, information about the tenant and asked a surveyor to check each property within a day and advise on any serious conditions.

Finally, on auction day, Mrs Elmer had identified the maximum she was going to bid for the properties that she had investigated. On the day, Mrs Elmer managed to secure another buy-to-let property and has now been managing the property for some years, along with the same tenant, who was happy to stay.

Ideally, you will want the agreements to be assured shorthold (see page 131) as these give you, as landlord, the most rights to your property and are the agreements most lenders will request anyway.

However, if it isn't an assured shorthold tenancy, you and your legal company will need to make further checks, such as whether you control the rent levels or have to refer them to a 'rent officer' as the tenants are covered by a protected, statutory or ordinary assured tenancy (see page 128).

Final checks include the landlord having no arrears on their mortgage payments and hasn't been issued with any notices from the lender. You also need confirmation that the local authority hasn't served any notices to upgrade the property in any way.

'The existing contracts with the tenants is the crux of whether the purchase is a sound investment or not.'

Furnished versus unfurnished

One of the main decisions you need to make when you are buying to let is whether you are going to let a property furnished or unfurnished.

There are advantages in both, the first being that if you let unfurnished, you don't have to go to the expense of buying furniture for the property in the first place! However, you are still likely to have to provide carpets and appliances, such as a cooker and washing machine (see the table, opposite).

In the main, whether you choose to let property with or without furniture is really down to what type of market you are aiming to target. If it is the higher value, shorter-term market, such as company lets, then you are likely to be expected to let the property furnished. However, if it is a family home, tenants may prefer to bring their own furniture for familiarity and potentially to save on storing it.

You can part furnish so you provide the basics such as beds, wardrobes, a settee, etc., and leave the tenants to provide whatever else they wish within the home.

Alternatively, you could give tenants the choice, they could pay a higher rent and deposit for a fully furnished property versus a property where they have to provide the furnishings for themselves.

With the growth in buy to let over the last ten years in the UK, there are alternatives to buying furniture.

- **For example,** you can rent furniture from companies on a short- or long-term basis.
- **Furnishings stores** like Ikea or some of your local shops might be happy to give you a 'package' deal to furnish your property.

See below for some useful websites.

'You have the choice of letting unfurnished, part-furnished or fully furnished, depending on what market you are aiming at.'

Useful websites for funishing a property include **www.davidphillips.com** and **www.roomservicebycort.com**. For a quick calculator to help you cost the items listed opposite, out go to **www.propertychecklists.co.uk**.

Pros and cons of letting property furnished versus unfurnished

	Furnished	Unfurnished
Property rent	■ Typically earn up to 5% more rent	■ Typically gain less rent, but depends on furnishing
Property insurance	■ Higher as you will need to insure the items within contents insurance	■ May only need to take out building insurance as opposed to contents insurance
Rentability	■ Often required with some lets and may mean the difference between someone taking the property or not	■ Can be an advantage for some who intend to buy a property later, or are renting temporarily so that they can fit in their own furniture and don't have to pay any storage costs
Expense	■ Costs around £1,500 to furnish a one-bed, £2,500 for a two-bed and £5,000 or more if it is a premium let ■ Benefit from a wear and tear allowance of 10% of the 'net rent'	■ Save on this investment, but need to weigh up the lower rent received and whether your target market will be happy furnishing themselves or buying their own furniture to fit

Checklist for furnishing a property

	Essential	Recommended
Kitchen*	Cooker Washing machine Kettle Fridge/freezer	Microwave Dishwasher Toaster/coffee maker
Also choose whether you provide crockery such as plates, cups, bowls, cutlery, cooking utensils, pots and pans		
Lounge	Settee Chairs	Coffee/side table TV cabinet
Dining room	Dining table Dining chairs	Sideboard/dresser
Bedroom	Bed Wardrobe	Bedside table Chest of drawers Desk
Bathroom	Cabinet Toilet holder/brush	
Within some of the rooms you may also need to provide additional lighting, such as lamps.		

* Make sure all appliances meet safety rules and regulations, for example are Portable Appliance Tested (PAT).

Renovating or building to let

To try to gain a better return on investment, some people are now looking at building or renovating to let. Before taking the plunge, follow the suggestions on pages 36–9 to ensure that you can let the property once finished.

Renovating to let

The key difference in renovating to let is that you will have to check out what building regulations will apply to the property and carefully check the cost of renovating the property before you make your offer. In the main, if the property requires just improving to a legally let standard – for example, new windows or doors – then few regulations will apply. However, if you are planning major alterations to the structure of the building or the drainage – such as removing a load-bearing wall – then you will need to check the specific building regulations that apply to you.

You will also need to ensure that the changes you make include any legal requirements for letting to the market that you have chosen.

'If you are planning major alterations to the structure of the building or the drainage, check the building regulations.'

With regard to your choice of fixtures and fittings, invest heavily where it saves you long term on maintenance and invest only to a required level where you are likely to have to replace or repair on a regular basis. Bear in mind the 'What you need to provide' information for different types of let on pages 22–34.

Don't forget that any increase in the cost of the renovation will affect your final yield (see pages 42–5), so it really does pay to make sure that the cost of the renovation adds enough to the property value. Even better would be if the renovation improves the property value sufficiently to ensure you gain a return.

Building to let

The first thing that you need to do is to find a plot of land to build on or a plot with a property that you can pull down. Ideally, you should find land that already has outline or detailed planning permission, unless you are prepared to take some months or years to get planning permission and for your invested money to give you a good return.

Where to look

This partly depends on where you are planning to build. There are certain areas that are more likely to have plots than others. For example, there is not much for sale in central London but areas such as Yorkshire and Lincolnshire have relatively plentiful plots available.

Wherever you decide to locate your build to let, then you will need to spend as much time as possible looking for a plot and ideally have your finances in order before you make an offer as competition for good plots tends to be high.

- **Auction houses:** It is worth checking out the local auctions to see what is available over, say, three months. This will give you an idea about how competitive a market you will be working in as well as where the plots are typically coming up. Perhaps you can get hold of some 'back catalogues' from the auction house, or if they are an estate agent, too (as is often the case), then you could ask them what land has become available and the average price per square metre and get an idea of how much it will cost you to buy your ideal plot. To find out more, visit www.eigroup.co.uk.
- **Internet searches:** There are some good database online search engines, such as: www.plotsearch. co.uk, which you can subscribe to. They cost around £50 to £100 to register but are good for researching across a range of areas. It can also save you lots of time driving around as some have aerial photographs that allow you to get a good view of the plots and their surroundings.

With any database make sure:

- **They show you** how many plots are available in each area before you buy so that you do not waste your money.
- **They are clear** about what planning permission has been given or what is required.
- **They update and validate** the plots regularly, so that they are truly available, rather than having been sold months ago.
- **They list what services** are available on the land as this can be expensive to provide if not already there.

Finally, search the local newspapers, trawl the estate agents, and drive around looking for potential plots. It is always worth talking to friends and family, too, as someone may have a large back garden they are willing to part with, or know someone who is looking to

BE CAREFUL!

If you are building on a plot, then you need to make sure it fits your target market - see pages 22-34 - and you need to measure the potential returns to ensure that you are making the right decision. For example, there may be more money to be made by building small two-bedroom properties for young professionals or newly weds than building a larger house with a student let in mind.

sell off some land, or has seen some land where you want to build.

The land

Check there is already outline or detailed planning permission. Even if you don't own the land, you can contact the local planning office to ask them for their view. Study the plans that have been submitted. You can't assume that the planning office will accept plans for apartments when they have given permission for a five-bedroomed house. Check with them first if you are looking to change the plans in any way. If necessary, you may need to get some help from a planning consultant to ensure:

- **There are no restrictions** on the land, such as preservation orders on trees or indeed on a building that is on the plot.
- **Whether the ground is sound** to build on. For example, you will need to know if the land is within 250m of a landfill site as this will require a special membrane before you build on it.

Check out the local environment

Check that this is suitable for your target market. If the area is a village, for example, and you are looking to build to rent to a family check that they can get into the local school, dentist or doctor's surgery, otherwise this may affect your ability to rent. Make sure, too, that there are good transport links for road, rail or airports.

How to assess the return

It is likely that if you go to the trouble of purchasing land and then building a property and renting it out, you are likely to gain a capital return as well as monies from rental income. In the past, building a home on a plot versus buying one 'already built' typically saved people around 30 per cent. Since the credit crunch, plots of land, for the short term, have become quite good value for money. If you are to make a good return out of building a property rather than buying and renting out, you need to be careful of the following figures before you make any offers:

- What price per square metre to pay for the land.
- Any costs to get services to the plot.
- Labour and material costs.
- Likely rental income.

Getting it right from the start is important as your build is likely to take a year or so before you can start earning money from letting the property, so you have to play 'catch up' versus buying a property already built, which you could have let straightaway.

Use the yield and return calculation on page 45 to assess whether it is worth buying a property to rent versus the one you are looking to build. For more information see the Which? book *Property Investor's Handbook*.

Letting a property

This chapter deals with the practicalities of letting, from managing it yourself to using an agent, dealing with tenants, and deciding when and how to upgrade your property.

Who will run the let?

Whether you choose to run the let yourself or through a letting agent (see pages 68–73), there are advantages and disadvantages. Read these pages and then make up your mind as to which you would prefer.

Doing it yourself

There are a number of good reasons for managing the let yourself rather than going straight to an agent, particularly if you are just starting out as a landlord. However, make sure you know what the disadvantages are before rushing in and then finding yourself on the wrong side of the law.

Advantages of self-managing

- **Saving money:** In the early days of any venture, money is often tight, and if you've just invested tens of thousands of pounds in a property, you want to start getting a decent return as soon as you can. You will be more motivated to keep costs to a minimum rather than use an agency, because it is your money you are saving. Managing it yourself will save you money because you won't have to pay a 'finder's fee' or an on-going management fee (see pages 68–73).
- **Learning the business:** There is no better way of learning how a business operates than by doing every job involved in it. You will learn what the most common problems are, how to deal with them, and what they cost. This will be valuable if you choose to bring in a manager or agent, because you will know as much as they do about your properties – and possibly more.
- **Making contacts:** Having people that you trust on hand to deal with the things you can't is invaluable. This might be a reliable plumber, a cheap, efficient handyman, or someone to hand over to when you have a holiday or your business expands.
- **Learning new skills:** Fixing things yourself is far cheaper than paying someone else to do it, and it can be interesting improving your DIY skills or facing new challenges. However, make sure you are aware of what repairs you can and can't make. For example, you now can't do major electrical work, nor can you do anything with regard to gas unless the gas engineer is on the Gas Safety Register.

Disadvantages of self-managing

- **Acting illegally:** There are so many new and changing laws in letting, from deposit protection and energy performance certificates to running HMOs (see pages 30–3), that you need to make sure you know what is required for your type of let. Join a landlord's association or consider using a letting specialist to let the property so you can benefit from their knowledge.
- **Time:** Dealing with the day-to-day running of a tenancy takes time. There is paperwork to keep on top of, much of it a legal requirement, and you will want to keep an eye on the property and deal with maintenance issues quickly to avoid antagonising your tenant. A useful calculation is to assess your time at the rate of pay and compare it to an estimate of how much time you will spend on landlord duties (including travel). You can then work out the cost of doing the job.
- **Location:** You can't manage a rental property from a distance, because you have to be on hand: it should preferably be fairly close to where you live and work.
- **Stress:** Tenants expect any problems to be dealt with fast and arranging that can involve a lot of hassle. You are on call at all times and you can, through no fault of you own, be put into stressful situations where there is conflict with the tenant; for example, if there are problems with their behaviour or if they don't pay the rent.
- **Lack of expertise:** If you don't know much about letting a property, it can be a steep and expensive learning curve. For example, repairing a leaking roof is an expensive job and if it isn't done right, you will be faced with an irate tenant and a damaged, damp property. Good landlords need to know quite a bit about repairs, and a lot about handling relationships with tenants and workmen. There are also legal issues on types of tenancy on which you should get professional advice. Finally, you'll have to deal with marketing the property, another drain on time and resources.

Helpful contacts

These organisations offer advice on being a landlord. Many are trade organisations that offer extra benefits and information to their members:

National Approved Letting Scheme:
www.nalscheme.co.uk

Royal Institution of Chartered Surveyors (RICS):
www.rics.org

UK Association of Letting Agents (UKALA):
www.ukala.org.uk

Association of Residential Letting Agents:
www.arla.co.uk

National Landlords Association:
www.landlords.org.uk, www.landlordzone.co.uk

Residential Landlords Association:
www.rla.org.uk

Residential Landlord:
www.residentiallandlord.co.uk

The Property Ombudsman: www.tpos.co.uk

Letting through an agent

Using a good agent will cost you a proportion of your rental income in return for saving you a lot of trouble. A bad one will take the money but not provide the service. Most agents offer three different services. 'Tenant find' is usually charged as a one-off fee, costing £300+. 'Letting only' is a fee, plus a percentage of the first month's rent, for example 5 per cent or more, and 'full management' costs from 10 per cent or 15 per cent plus in London.

- **Tenant find only:** The agent will market and carry out viewings and recommend a tenant. It's your responsbility to organise tenant referencing, check in and to manage the let.
- **Letting only:** The letting agent will look after the tenant until the time that he or she has moved into the property.
- **Full management:** The agent is primarily responsible for finding and checking in and checking out the tenant as well as managing both the tenant and the property.

BE CAREFUL!

On top of the commission on rent, agencies may also charge landlords:

- **An administration fee at the start of the tenancy.**
- **A renewal fee every time a tenant renews their contract.**
- **A fee for carrying out an inventory.**
- **Some agents charge advertising costs.**

Advantages of letting through an agent

- **They know the market:** A good agent can advise you on preparing your property for the right market so that you have the best chance of letting it. A good agent will also be able to advise on what rent you can charge.
- **Legal responsibilities:** If you have a good letting agent, they will know the legal rules and regulations, keeping your property and you up to date and fully within the law. They can also keep your costs down if they negotiate favourable rates for insurance and maintenance issues.
- **They take care of marketing:** Finding reliable tenants is the trickiest aspect of the rental market and a good agent will save you the trouble of doing it. Their expertise should also help you to minimise the dreaded void periods when you have no tenant and therefore no income. Tenants looking for larger properties, and corporate clients, tend to expect to deal with professional agents.
- **They have the expertise:** If you are starting out as a landlord, you can learn a lot through employing a good agent so that if you choose to go it alone or save outgoings by taking on some of the responsibilities, you will have a better grasp of what to do.

- **You don't have to deal with tenants:** An agent can be a very useful buffer between you and your tenants. This is particularly helpful if you get one who is difficult to deal with, or if you do not relish handling dealing directly with tenants.
- **The agent will deal with any repairs:** Stuck for a plumber or a roofing contractor? A good agent won't be.
- **They will deal with the money:** Having an agent handle money is simpler and takes away the responsibility of dealing with the deposit (see box on page 73).

Disadvantages of letting through an agent

- **Money:** Fees vary, but they will charge a percentage of your rent plus other fees for renewing contracts or finding new tenants (see opposite). Agents can also deal with sorting out repairs, but while some will have negotiated discounts to give you a good deal, others will make additional charges, including their own fees.

Read the contract

You must always read the contract and make sure that you understand the small print before signing it. Terms to check on include:

- **The length of notice to cancel.** One to three months for either side is typical, but some agents will ask for more.
- **Any fees** that will be charged by the agent in addition to the commission on rents.
- **Exactly what the agent will deal with,** for example, chasing arrears and handling repairs.
- **Charging for periods** when there are no tenants – this is acceptable only if you are on a full management contract.
- **A 'sold fee'** if you put the house up for sale and the tenant buys it.

For more details on these points and additional information on a terms of business agreement with an agent, see pages 200–5. Ideally, check the agreement with a lettings legal specialist.

Scrutinising agent charges

There are many fees that letting agents charge and they also vary depending on where you live. Some offer great 'headline' fees, but then you find you are paying for everything else on top, so to help compare agents' charges and understand what costs you will incur see the points outlined below.

- Ask for a single page document that highlights all the charges made.
- Request a cost per hour if you want help with things not included on the list, like going to court on your behalf.
- Always compare agent fees over a 12 month period, including a tenancy renewal.

Key questions to ask a letting agent

- Will you give a valuation and advice on a property before purchase?
- Are you a member of a trade body?
- If not, why not?
- If you are, can I see the code of conduct and what happens in case of a dispute?
- How do you keep up with the legal rules and regulations of letting?
- How many properties similar to mine do you have available for rent?
- How many are currently NOT being let – and for how long?
- How long does it usually take from advertising to gaining a tenant?
- How many viewings normally need to take place – and do you do this as part of your fee or not?
- Have you anyone currently looking for my type of property?
- Will you advertise the property in the local paper and in your window – using pictures or just text?
- What online websites do you advertise on?
- What qualifications have you/your staff got in letting?
- Can you provide a copy of your fees, charges and services and your terms and conditions of business?
- Can you give me a copy of your contract between a tenant and your agency (you should then check this with your own lawyer)?
- If there are issues raised by the tenant, how would you deal with them? (Would they just pass the problem to you or try to resolve it first?)
- What happens if the tenant leaves before the end of their agreement?
- What happens if the tenant doesn't pay up?
- What happens over repairs to the home?
- What tenant checks are carried out?
- How long does it take from the tenant paying to it appearing in my bank account?
- If you go bust, will I get any outstanding rent back?
- If you do the repairs, am I charged at cost? If there's a mark-up, how much is it?
- If there is a discrepancy over the inventory report between you and the inventory company, how will this be handled by the letting agent?

Choosing an agent

The good news is that there are about 8,000 letting agents in the UK who are members of trade bodies, which offer some kind of protection. The bad news is that that leaves possibly as many as 9,000 agents who are not regulated at all, working in a growing market with high demand in which people are likely to enthusiastically sign up to let their new home without checking the small print, which sometimes has outrageous clauses hidden away.

Always go for an agent who is a member of the National Approved Letting Scheme (NALS) or belongs to one of the professional bodies such as the Association of Residential Letting Agents (ARLA), the Royal Institution of Chartered Surveyors (RICS) or the Property Ombudsman (TPOS) and the UK Association of Letting Agents (UKALA) (see box on page 67). Also make sure you opt for an agent who deals with the market you want to serve as they will have the expertise you need.

The reason this is so important is that there is a clear course of action if you have difficulties and can't come to a conclusion yourselves. This can be an invaluable time and money saver, just when you will need support and help if things are not working out.

NALS, ARLA or SafeAgent please

Members of the National Approved Letting Scheme (NALS) (which is government financed) have to abide by a code of conduct and must:

- Have a client's money protection scheme covering any landlord or tenant's monies misappropriated or lost by the agent.
- Be a member of a third-party complaints scheme.
- Operate an internal complaints procedure.
- Be linked to a legally binding arbitration service.
- Maintain professional indemnity insurance.

Agents who belong to www.safeagents.co.uk protect landlord and tenant money via an insurance called client money protection. The UK Association of Letting Agents has its own code of practice and also supports the NALS scheme.

BE CAREFUL!

To make sure you protect your rental payments or income, make sure the agent is a member of SafeAgent, which covers you with client money protection. Many estate agents are now operating lettings divisions due to a lack of sales. Be warned that they may well not be as up-to-date with letting legals and regulations or as good at essential lettings administration.

The relevant websites for the professional letting agency bodies are: **www.arla.co.uk** (ARLA); **www.tpos.co.uk**; **www.nalscheme.co.uk**, **www.rics.org** and **www.safeagents.co.uk**.

Letting through an accommodation agency

Accommodation agencies mainly aim at the student market, nursing, police and fire services, working in many cases in markets where price is all important. Some large companies with a big workforce also run what are, in effect, accommodation offices. Many higher educational establishments operate their own agency on-site. They often vet their landlords so that they meet certain minimum requirements, and can act as mediators in disputes.

Advantages of accommodation agencies

These agencies frequently make no charge to landlords, as they are paid by the tenant when they take on a property. Because they are often part of large organisations with many potential tenants, they are a major player in their local markets.

'Accommodation agencies filter information on what is available, mainly for students.'

Disadvantages of accommodation agencies

These agencies do not usually provide the fuller service a letting agent offers: they are really simply filters for information on what is available. University accommodation offices will list the accommodation offered by and through the university, including halls of residence and other properties owned by the university, and the recent trend for high quality dedicated student blocks available for quite reasonable rents, such as those offered by Unite (see www.unite-students.com). So they are marketing a range of competing properties. This is good for the tenant, who gets a wide choice of property, but makes the market more competitive for the landlord.

Letting via social rent

The market for social letting is described on pages 33–4. Social lets are for people on low income or Housing Benefit, and are provided by local authorities or housing associations, who also usually own the properties. However, such is the demand that private landlords can enter this market. Local authorities vet private landlords carefully and can decide and cap the rent they charge. Housing associations also have clear requirements, but will often manage the property themselves for a very reasonable fee.

Advantages of social lets

For a landlord, a social let has a number of benefits:

- **Guaranteed rental income** on long leases if the LHA (see page 150) is paid directly to the landlord.
- **Low fees** for what is, in effect, often a full management service (see page 68).
- **Often there is an optional repairs** and maintenance service.
- **Cheaper insurance** through the organisation.
- **The satisfaction of making an ethical investment** in social housing, which helps the disadvantaged.

Disadvantages of social lets

- **Some lenders forbid landlords from letting** to these groups (and some landlords choose not to), partly because Housing Benefit/LHA (or, from 2013, Universal Credit) regulations can result in the landlord being held responsible for large financial liabilities incurred by the tenant if, for example, they are found to have been claiming benefit fraudulently or have been overpaid by the local authority.
- **Council rent officers have powers** to limit the amount of rent charged to ensure tenants are treated fairly.

Local Housing Allowance (LHA)

Housing Benefit is no longer typically paid directly to the landlord and some tenants don't pass the allowance monies onto the landlord. This has led to an estimated £4,000+ arrears for some landlords. Some local authorities help resolve the situation, some don't. Find out more about your local housing officer's attitude towards private sector rentals/landlords.

An alternative to a deposit

Because people on benefits often cannot afford to pay a deposit, some councils make a one-off, non-returnable fee to landlords who start letting to tenants on benefit. The fee is typically £1,000–£1,750, depending on the size of the property.

The local authority will vet the property to ensure it is of a reasonable standard and set a reasonable rent. They will then introduce potential tenants to the landlord, who can vet and choose them in the usual way.

The authority does not manage the property or act as guarantor for the tenant, but it will provide a shorthold tenancy agreement. Essentially, this fee is a down payment on any damage or loss the landlord may incur when letting to tenants on benefit.

Preparing the property

As a landlord you are bound by the law to ensure that the property you let is safe for people to live in. As well as gas, electricity and fire safety, this includes various insurances.

Safety first

There are many laws that you need to abide by and these cover anything from gas and electricty safety through to the Data Protection Act (see pages 76–7).

Gas

The Gas Safety (Installation and Use) Regulations 1998 require landlords to ensure that all gas appliances are maintained in good order and that an annual safety check is carried out by a tradesman who is registered with the Gas Safe Register. You must keep a record of the safety checks and issue it to the tenant within 28 days of each annual check. Although not a legal requirement, you may also choose to install carbon monoxide detectors. Some student accommodation offices have a stock of detectors so tenants can check levels of this invisible and odourless gas.

Electricity

You are legally obliged to ensure the electrical system and any electrical appliances you supply, such as cookers, kettles, washing machines and immersion heaters, are safe to use. While it is not a legal requirement, a check on electrical equipment prior to the start of the tenancy, and annually thereafter, will reassure you and your tenant. Use a member of the National Inspection Council for Electrical Installation Contracting (NICEIC), National Association for Professional Inspectors and Testers (NAPIT) or the Electrical Contractor Association (ECA). It is a legal requirement to employ only qualified people to carry out major electrical work, such as installing an electric shower.

Fire safety

Any furniture and furnishings you supply must meet the fire resistance

For safety advice, go to **www.gassaferegister.co.uk**, **www.carbonmonoxidekills.com**, **www.gov.uk** (search for 'fire safety in your home') and **www.shelter.org.uk**. ARLA (**www.arla.co.uk**) supplies a leaflet for landlords on safety.

requirements in the Furniture and Furnishings (Fire) (Safety) Regulations 1988. These set levels of fire resistance for domestic upholstered furniture. All new and second-hand furniture provided in accommodation that is let for the first time, or replacement furniture in existing let accommodation, must meet the fire resistance requirements unless it was made before 1950. Most furniture will have a manufacturer's label on it saying if it meets the requirements.

Smoke alarms

All properties built after June 1992 must have a mains-operated, inter-connected smoke alarm fitted on every level of the property. Older properties do not meet this requirement, but you should provide battery-operated smoke alarms in suitable locations for your and your tenants' peace of mind. It is reasonable to ask the tenant to check these regularly and inform you of any problems. A good tip is to put new batteries in the smoke alarms when the tenant moves in or ideally have them connected to the mains.

BE CAREFUL!

A booklet called A Guide to the Furniture and Furnishings (Fire) (Safety) Regulations can be downloaded from www.bis.gov.uk.

Other responsibilities

The landlord is responsible for the structure and exterior of the property and must also ensure that all hot and cold water supplies, and the drains, are properly maintained.

Insurance

Landlords cannot rely on standard household insurance policies, which can be invalidated if the property is let out. Insurers regard rental property as a greater risk than other residences, especially those that are HMOs or occupied by students or Housing Benefit tenants, and consequently charge higher premiums for it. You should ensure your policy includes:

- **Property owner's liability,** which covers for death, injury or damage to anyone on the property, including tenants, their guests and other visitors.

Appliances

Because of the safety regulations on appliances supplied by landlords, keep the number of appliances you provide for tenants to a minimum. If they really want a dishwasher or washing machine, they can hire one (unless, of course, you are seeking a corporate let). Leave written instructions on how to operate any appliances you provide: what may seem obvious to you may not be so clear to someone else. All appliances should ideally be portable appliance tested (PAT).

If your tenants are students or on Housing Benefit, the university or local authority will specify a minimum amount of cover. This 'third party' cover is often overlooked by landlords, at potentially great cost.

- **Cover for employers' liability** for a handyman, decorator or gardener who is injured on the property.
- **Insure only the property** that belongs to you, either the cheaper 'limited contents cover' or 'full contents cover', which is generally worthwhile if the contents are valued at more than £5,000.
- **Also consider paying for emergency assistance insurance** to cover urgent repairs – this is particularly valuable if you live a long way from the property you are letting out.
- **Cover for damage** caused by the tenants either accidentally or maliciously.
- **Other possible elements of cover** are for rent guarantee (which reduces the risk of losing money through bad payers and is more attractive to small-scale landlords) and legal expenses insurance, because solicitors are not cheap.

You should also protect your investment by taking out buildings insurance in case the property is damaged. This covers you for the cost of re-building the property. Specialist landlord's policies will also cover you for loss of rent while re-building work is in progress. Some policies have the option of cover for malicious damage caused by the tenants.

BE CAREFUL!

Some companies offer cheap insurance for landlords which, when push comes to shove, you find doesn't really cover you for anything at all. Make sure you have good insurance cover or it could cost you thousands. If you are letting through an agency, you may be able to secure a comprehensive insurance policy more cheaply. Buying this makes your life easier as you then know you are covered for most problems that might occur.

Data protection

Landlords often hold private information about their tenants, such as references, a list of who is claiming benefit, and if they are not paying their rent. The Data Protection Act 1998 sets out who they can pass this information on to.

- **A landlord can pass on** the names of new tenants to utility companies, and should tell individuals this may happen when they agree the tenancy.

More information about data protection can be found from the Information Commissioner's Office at **www.ico.gov.uk** or tel 0303 123 1113. Click on the relevant tab where there are several links to different parts of the website.

- **Landlords are entitled to see tenant references** given to their letting agent, provided the agent made it clear to tenant and referee that this would happen.
- **Landlords cannot display a list** of tenants in arrears.
- **If a tenant does not pay the rent,** the landlord can pass on their details to a tracing agent or debt collection company. It is good practice to include this information in the tenancy agreement.

General good practice for data protection is to consider:

- Whether the information in question is personal.
- Whether you have told the tenants you may give out the information.
- Who wants the information and why it is wanted.
- Whether you are legally obliged to give it.
- Whether it is necessary to give it.

Who else needs to know?

When letting a property, it is important to inform these organisations:

- **Your lender.** If the rental property is mortgaged, you must get the lender's consent to let it. Without this consent, the lender has the right to demand full repayment of the loan and ultimately to take possession of the property and sell it to recover its money. Request consent in writing. Lenders normally agree as long as the tenant is to have no security of tenure. Some lenders charge a fee for considering the application and giving consent. Others give consent subject to a 0.25 or 0.5 per cent increase on the loan rate. In this case, it may be worth seeking independent financial advice to make sure that staying with your current lender is viable.

Identity theft

Landlords are particularly vulnerable to identity fraud because their tenants will have access to their personal details and may well have opportunities to intercept mail, especially if the landlord once lived at the property now being let. Measures that will reduce the risk to landlords are:

- When you move out, have your post re-directed by Royal Mail, rather than returning to pick it up.
- Remove yourself from direct mail listings at the rental address through the Mailing Preference Service (www.mpsonline.org.uk).
- Provide individual mail boxes for tenants who are sharing a property.
- Check your financial statements and credit reference regularly.

Bodies such as the National Landlords Association (**www.landlords.org.uk**) offer insurance for landlords and **www.landlordzone.co.uk** has links to many insurers. The Association of British Insurers at **www.abi.org.uk**, **www.homelet.co.uk** and local lettings specialists may have good value, bespoke insurance.

Housing Health and Safety Rating System

Local authorities have the right to inspect any residential property to check on its safety. The Housing Health and Safety Rating System (HHSRS), introduced in England and Wales in 2006, applies a hazard rating to private and public sector dwellings. The most common hazards are cold, fire, falls, lead in drinking water pipes and old paintwork, and hot surfaces that could scald. Inspectors can visit any property, most probably prompted by the concerns of a tenant, and can insist on repairs being carried out, backed by the threat of a £5,000 fine for non-compliance. This system replaces the Housing Fitness Standard, set out in the Housing Act 1985. Further guidance is available from www.communities.gov.uk/documents/housing/pdf/150940.pdf. HHSRS can be interpreted differently at a local level, so make sure you understand what is required by your local authority.

- **The local authority finance department,** which deals with Council Tax.
- **If the property is a house in multiple occupation (HMO),** your local authority may have an HMO Registration Scheme with which you have to register (see page 31).
- **The neighbours.** They may need to contact you about the tenants, and, if you have a good relationship, may let you know if they spot any potential maintenance problem.

Viewings

It is particularly important that you prepare the property carefully for viewing. Check it is clean and tidy, making sure all the lights work and there are no obvious flaws like a dripping tap.

- **Have someone with you** for security, or at least tell a friend or colleague the time of the visit and when you will be back.
- **Tidy the garden/exterior.**
- **Wash the front door.**
- **Tidy any communal areas,** such as a hallway.
- **Check the kitchen** for cleanliness and smells, including hidden parts, such as grills and microwave interiors.
- **If you are furnishing the property,** cover bare mattresses with a throw or blanket – it gives a much more homely impression. It may even be worth dressing the rooms with, say, some pictures and a vase of flowers for a better 'homely' feel.
- **Air the property** thoroughly, and sort out any sources of smells, such as a blocked drain.
- **Have all relevant information handy,** including estimated running costs.
- **Check you've got keys** to all areas/rooms.

Entering into a contract

Before entering into the contract, it is important you do some basic tenancy checks to establish that your potential tenant is who he says he is and also has a good credit record. You don't want to be left with a non-payer on your hands.

Tenancy checks

When you have a vacant property, you naturally want to let it as soon as possible. However, it is vital to carry out checks on every tenant before offering them a tenancy: an empty property is less hassle than a problem tenant, and you can lose more money through having a bad tenant than a void period. The ideal tenant will:

- Pay their rent on time.
- Respect and look after the property.
- Be a good neighbour.
- Probably want to renew the lease.

Someone like this is unlikely to cause you financial and emotional stress, so it is worth investing some time in screening out the tenants who don't match these criteria. Part of this will be gut instinct: do you want to deal with this person and have them living in your property? You can start to do this over the phone – the most likely first point of contact. Have a checklist prepared for each conversation, covering the items listed to the right.

- Name.
- Address (and if they are currently renting, contact number for the landlord or agent).
- Landline and mobile numbers.
- Reason for moving.
- Job (including name of employer) or course (if in higher education).
- Date accommodation required, and preferred length of lease.
- Number of people who will be living in the property and if this includes children.
- Do they smoke?

Tenants with children and pets

There are many horror stories of dogs, cats and, unfortunately, children causing untold damage to carpets, curtains, paintwork, the garden and other fixtures and fittings. This can cause issues as it may take a few weeks for you to repair the damage to the property and you may lose the income rather than let straightaway. However, some landlords are happy to let to tenants with pets and children and allow smoking in their property.

Visit Lets with Pets to find out about letting safely to pet owners: www.letswithpets.org.uk.

- Do they have pets?
- Can they supply a reference?

This will give you a good start in assessing how trustworthy the person is. If they view the property and are interested, ask them to fill in an application form, which gathers more information on their background (see below).

Identity check

When you meet the tenant, ask to see their passport or other proof of identity, and note down its details. Take a note of any vehicle licence plate numbers they turn up in.

Credit check

A credit check will identify people with a bad credit record or with County Court Judgements against them. The main credit reference agencies are Experian (www.experian.co.uk), Equifax (www.equifax.co.uk) and Callcredit (www.callcredit.co.uk), providing they have given you correct identity information. There is a charge per check, so you will want to keep these to a minimum, and may, with their agreement, pass the cost on to the tenant.

No record

Remember that not everyone has a credit record: many students, for example, have not built one up by the time they need accommodation. In these cases, it makes sense to ensure they can provide a reliable guarantor, who will need to be vetted in the same way as the tenant. Credit checking is also tricky for people from overseas, and it would be very difficult to pursue an overseas guarantor. However, if they have a job, their employer may be prepared to do it. An alternative is to ask for the rent to be paid for the length of the contract in advance.

'When it comes to making all these checks you can't be too careful - make them all just to be on the safe side.'

Financial and/or character reference

If the person has a job, a reference from their employer will confirm their financial stability and give you some idea of their character. Write, ring and check the premises of the employer yourself rather than accept a letter handed over by the tenant (they are easy to forge). Secure three months of

You can download an application form free from **www.landlordzone.co.uk**, or members of the Residential Landlords Association can go to **www.rla.org.uk**.

bank statements to make sure they can afford the rent. Check when they are paid and make sure your rent comes to you first, not last when they are struggling with their budget. For those with jobs, the three most recent salary slips will show how much salary is being paid in each month.

Rental history

If they have rented before, ask for details of their previous landlord or letting agency. A phone call, letter or even a visit will establish if they paid regularly and what condition they kept and left the property in.

Your decision

A landlord has the legal right to choose which tenant to let to, provided the decision is based on legitimate business criteria and complies with anti-discrimination laws. If you are accepting the tenant, wait until the checks are complete and inform them promptly. If you are rejecting them, do so promptly and politely explain the reason. Keep a record of your evidence in case you are accused of discrimination.

BE CAREFUL!

Sadly there are bad tenants who are practised in obtaining accommodation when they have no intention of paying rent regularly. They know how the letting process works and tend to avoid large, professional letting companies in preference for small-scale landlords. This is because such landlords don't necessarily have the experience or the resources to vet their tenants thoroughly.

Screen test

Specialist tenant screening companies (see below) will carry out a number of checks on potential tenants. This can save a lot of time and effort, but, of course, they will charge for their service.

The contract

You must have an up-to-date legal agreement with the tenant. If you fail to do this, there is enormous potential for confusion and conflict later on, even if you are only renting a room out to a friend. Never hand over the keys before this agreement is signed.

All agreements post 1997 are known as assured shorthold tenancies (see pages 131) unless otherwise specified. They should be signed by you, as landlord, the tenant(s) and, if there is one, a present guarantor, plus an independent witness (see page 200).

Specialist tenant screening companies can be found at **www.tenantverify.co.uk** and **www.fccparagon.com**. For more contract information, see **www.experian.com/screening-services/tenant-screening-services/** and pages 190–204.

If you are using a letting agency, they'll have a standard contract – but make sure any special clauses you need have been correctly added – even a tiny mistake can invalidate a clause.

You can ask a solicitor to draw up the contract (choose one who has experience in letting legals), but you can also buy standard contracts from legal stationers or order online from suppliers, such as www.legalhelpers.co.uk, www.clickdocs.co.uk or www.letlink.co.uk. There are also sample clauses given on pages 190–204. Either the landlord pays for the contract, or you share the cost of preparing the tenancy agreement. Of course, once you have bought one agreement you can use it for all your subsequent tenants. Whatever contract you use, make sure you keep up to date as recommended by the company you purchased it from.

BE CAREFUL!

If your tenant has children or pets or they smoke, you might want to ensure that you (or your legal representative) has put clauses in the contract regarding any damage to the property caused by the pet/child/smoking. These may include 'making good' the damage to your satisfaction prior to leaving or to the satisfaction of an independent inventory check. Perhaps a higher deposit would be advisable, just in case.

How will you be paid?

Clarify at the outset how the rent will be paid. If you are using an agent, they'll handle this. If not, a standing order to your bank account is the most reliable. Try to avoid regular visits to collect cash, for security reasons, and because there is always the danger the tenant will try to delay payment or say they can't pay in full this time. If the tenant writes you a cheque, allow time for it to be cleared by their bank - usually three working days. If you agree to be paid weekly, by law, you must provide the tenant with a rent book and fill this in every week when the money is sent or collected.

Setting the rent

The key when setting a rent for new or existing tenants is to be realistic and follow the market rate: a month's void while you are marketing the property at a higher rent will cost more than the increased income you are trying to bring in. LHA that is used for social rents is set lower than average local rents – visit www.voa.gov.uk for more information on LHA rent levels. See page 154 for legal obligations when setting the rent.

For more information on the background to different agreements, see pages 128–34. The chapter on assured shorthold tenancies is on pages 136–48.

The deposit

The deposit, or rather its return, has traditionally been a source of dispute between tenants and landlords.

It is essential to take a deposit to cover the cost of any damage to the property or its furniture found at the end of the let. It is usually equivalent to four to six weeks' rent (the average deposit ranges from £750 to just over £1,000, according to Mydeposits) and must be paid before the tenant moves in. A deposit can cause problems because:

- **Tenants feel deductions** have been made unfairly, when the property has not been left in poor condition.
- **Tenants withhold payment of rent** at the end of the tenancy on the assumption that the deposit covers their rental payments.

However, in England and Wales since April 2007 and 2012 new legislation requires deposits to be protected in an independent third-party scheme. It applies to properties rented under an assured shorthold tenancy agreement (AST) in England and Wales and when rent is less than £100,000 per annum. It deems that any landlord taking a deposit must safeguard it with a tenancy deposit protection scheme.

Any tenant must be notified via the tenancy agreement or by a letter within 30 days of the tenancy to confirm the deposit is protected and by which company and the type of scheme. If this isn't done, a landlord may not be able to serve a Section 21 possession notice (see page 163), and may be penalised with a fine of between one and three times the deposit. The tenant should also get the contact details of the scheme and guidance on what to do if there is a disagreement.

About the schemes

- **Custodial scheme.** This is where the tenant pays the deposit money to the landlord/agent and it is then passed to the scheme itself. It is free for landlords/agents to use as the interest generated by the deposits pays for the scheme.
- **Insurance-based scheme.** In this instance, the tenant pays the deposit to the landlord or agent, who keeps the deposit (and any interest payable) and pays a premium to the insurer.

There is one custodial scheme, The Deposit Protection Service (The DPS), and there are four insurance-based schemes: My Deposits (formerly the Tenancy Deposit Solutions Ltd), Tenancy Deposit

Visit **www.communties.gov.uk** for tenancy deposit FAQs and for tenancy deposit protection schemes, go to **www.depositprotection.com/**, **www.mydeposits.co.uk/**, **www.thedisputeservice.co.uk/** and **www.capita-tdp.co.uk**.

Rogue landlords

Rogue landlords tend to offer to take two months' rent but no deposit, so make sure you always inform tenants that a deposit should be taken. If you have had a tenant since April 2007 and don't protect their deposit in a scheme, the tenant can report you to the local Crown Court. Ideally never use a landlord that won't take, or doesn't protect, your deposit, unless you are renting a room.

Scheme (TDS), and Capita and the Deposit Protection Service have launched their own scheme.

If things go wrong

If all parties agree, information concerning the dispute is collated by the scheme. This information is then typically considered by an independent case adjudicator.

Are the schemes working?

The schemes have received mixed reviews since they started. On the one hand, they have built enormous costs into the system while the expected number of disputes has been far less than originally predicted. On the other hand, the organisations that back the schemes suggest that low dispute numbers mean the system is working! Figures from The DPS from 2011 suggest that the dispute levels are reasonably even, with less than 1 per cent of their 870,000 deposits going to dispute. Of the 6,056 disputes, 16 per cent of claimants were awarded in favour of the landlord, 36 per cent in favour of the tenants and 48 per cent were split between the landlord and tenant.

Top tips for avoiding disputes

As a landlord, you can never rule out a potential dispute, but follow these tips and help yourself to avoid them:

- Ensure there is a thorough check in and out of reports, which is signed by both parties.
- Use photos as evidence of the property, both before and after.
- Send or request instructions of what the tenant should do/leave at the property.

No deposits

Tenants sometimes struggle to find the money for a deposit. If the problem is lack of funds, a guarantor may be able to provide them.
A common problem is that they are still waiting for the return of their last deposit when they want to rent your property. In such cases, try contacting their previous landlord: you may be able to hurry along the money and get a reference. As a general point, if the tenant is struggling to find the deposit and can't secure a guarantor, this doesn't bode well for the future, so you might want to choose a different tenant.

- Make sure all communication, particularly deposit related, is in writing.
- Include everything required by the schemes when disputing a deposit.

The inventory

It is in the interest of both landlord and tenant to agree exactly what is in the property at the start of the tenancy and, crucially, its condition, so that you will both know if anything is missing or damaged. Sometimes known as a schedule of condition, the inventory should list items (including the carpets, fixtures and fittings) room by room. This document is as vital as the tenancy agreement: it will provide evidence to indicate whether or not money should be deducted from the deposit, and it is valuable as a record of contents for insurance purposes.

If you carry out the inventory (it can be time-consuming), create a document with four columns: item, condition, comments and final inspection.

- **Note the make, model and serial number** of any electrical goods (this is also useful for insurance purposes).
- **Be specific about any faults:** for example, note 'fridge light not working' on the inventory rather than 'fridge faulty'.
- **Make sure you write legibly** (not always easy when you are moving from room to room, but use a clipboard and take your time).

For an idea of the sort of items that will be included in each room, see page 86.

Ideally, the tenant should be present when the inventory is checked, and in any case they should make sure they agree with

BE CAREFUL!

If you let the property via an agent and use their inventory company to carry out the checks, make sure you know which party is responsible for any errors. For example, if the inventory company ticks to say something is there and you then find it isn't, check that the letting agent/ inventory association will sort the dispute out for you and don't sign the inventory until you are happy it is correct. If it requires legal action, know before you agree to use them whether you would take action against the inventory company or the agent that employs them.

Using an independent company shows you value your property and contents. The Association of Independent Inventory Clerks specialises in inventories: **www.theaiic.co.uk**. See **www.theinventorymanager.co.uk** for online inventories. If a dispute arises, go to **www.depositprotection.com** for a free guide.

Inventory table for each room

Choose the appropriate items from these suggestions to make your own inventory. Once created, the inventory can be adapted and reused for each tenant.

Kitchen

Door
Windows/locks
Lighting
Flooring
Curtains/blinds
Oven/hob
Microwave
Kettle
Toaster
Fridge and/or fridge freezer
Washing machine
Dishwasher
Sink and taps
Iron/ironing board
Crockery
Cutlery

Bathroom

Door
Windows/locks
Lighting
Flooring
Curtains/blinds
Bathtub
Shower/shower curtain
Toilet
Sink
Cabinet
Mirror
Toilet roll holder
Towel rail
Other fittings
Extractor fan

Living room

Door
Windows/locks
Lighting
Flooring
Curtains/blinds
Sofa
Chairs
Table(s)
Shelves
Cupboards
Fireplace

Bedroom

Door
Windows/locks
Lighting
Flooring
Curtains/blinds
Bed
Table
Wardrobe
Chest of drawers

Hallway/stairs

Door
Windows/locks
Lighting
Flooring
Curtains/blinds
Fire extinguisher
Thermostat
Boiler

Floor flaws

One of the most common reasons for dispute is when a landlord says the carpets or other floor coverings have been left in such a bad state they need replacing. This is particularly frequent if the tenant kept a pet in the house. Always check flooring in hidden areas, such as under sofas and, if possible, take photographs or video of existing wear or damage.

all the information in the document before signing it. Date it and give a copy to the tenant.

You or your agent may choose to use an inventory company, in which case ensure the company is a member of the Association of Independent Inventory Clerks (www.theaiic.co.uk) as they offer third party resolution for any disputes that can't be settled.

Who pays?

Inventory costs can be borne by the landlord or shared by the tenant and landlord, so landlord and tenant pay half each, or sometimes landlords pay for the initial inventory and charge the tenant for the one conducted at the end of the tenancy.

Key point

Before you hand over the keys (and make sure you've got a set for each tenant), take the tenant on a detailed tour of the property, showing him or her where to find: the meters, the fuse box, the water stopcock, the boiler, central heating controls, smoke detectors and window lock keys.

Put all this in a folder with a copy of the agreement, contact details in emergencies, utility company information, guidance on how to operate the appliances and information on how and when the bins are emptied. Add to this a list of contacts for:

- **You:** landline and mobile numbers.
- **The agent,** if you have one.
- **A contact** if you are unavailable in an emergency.
- **A trusted plumber, gas fitter and electrician** in the event of an emergency when you cannot be reached. In the eventuality of the tenant paying for the work to be done, you would normally reimburse your tenant. Ideally, leave your insurance details with the tenant so it is all sorted properly.
- **It is a nice gesture** to give them a list of other useful contacts, such as the nearest doctor and details of bus and train services – much appreciated if the tenant is new to the area.

Before you leave, note down and even photograph all meter readings as paying these bills is the tenant's responsibility (unless you are operating a short-term let). You will then have relevant information to hand if there is a problem and the utility company contacts you.

Managing the let

Contented tenants pay the rent and are more likely to want to renew their agreement. This is a winning formula for landlords as they get a nice regular income with very low marketing costs.

There are a number of golden rules on being a good landlord:

- **Be available.** Either you or your agent must be ready to communicate. Some tenants won't want to pay for the extra expense of ringing a mobile number, so check your landline message system regularly. There is generally a four-to-six week teething period at the start of a tenancy after which things settle down.
- **Deal with repairs quickly.** Living with a leaking ceiling or a dodgy boiler is no fun, and tenants can become frustrated if repairs take a long time – giving them an incentive and a reason to withhold part of the rent in compensation for the inconvenience. Using the same reliable workmen all the time builds trust and commitment with them, too.
- **Respect the privacy of the tenant.** Don't 'pop in' on them: always give at least 24 hours' notice that you need to enter the property, and always use the doorbell, not your own key. See page 114 for guidance on when you are allowed to enter the property.
- **In all your dealings,** stay businesslike but friendly.
- **Visit fairly regularly, by appointment.** While the tenant will tell you if there is water coming through the roof, he might not notice a slow build-up of damp in a corner. Try to visit your property every three months, in daylight, and check it thoroughly as if you were looking to buy it. You (or if necessary, an experienced colleague) should spot any developing problems before they become serious. If you can see that problems are arising from the tenant's conduct, write to them with a warning that additional costs may be being incurred for

Despite best intentions, the time can come when a landlord needs to turn to the law for support. See pages 160–7 for how to take legal action. Grounds for possession are also included in that chapter on pages 168–71.

damage or cleaning beyond normal wear and tear.

- **Stay organised** with ongoing maintenance, such as getting the boiler serviced and the gas fittings checked. Write the due dates well ahead in your diary.
- **Keep notes of communication either way:** in a dispute over repairs it may be helpful to know the exact date or even time you were contacted.
- **Check your bank account regularly** and if the rent has not been paid, act immediately. It can take a few months to move out a tenant who turns out to be a bad payer (see pages 160–76) and the earlier you spot a problem and do something about it, the better.
- **Small kindnesses** can be worth a fortune in goodwill. Some landlords reward good tenants with gestures, such as paying their TV licence, for example, or upgrading something in the property without the tenant asking: it is much harder to fall out with people with whom you are on good terms, and the benefits work both ways (provided they pay the rent!).

Raising the rent

The cost of the rent will be set out in the contract and cannot be changed until it is time to negotiate a renewal. Be careful not to agree a long-term let of, say, two or three years without allowing for a rent review as the rent could stop bringing a good return and you won't be able to fund maintenance. Some agreements set out how any rent rise will be calculated, usually linked to changes in the consumer price index.

Renewing the contract

Tenants who renew their contracts are by far the easiest to manage: both parties know each other, and, provided the tenant is behaving within the terms of the agreement, there is every reason for you to renew the let and avoid a costly void and the trouble of finding and vetting a new occupant. If you are employing a letting agent, they are likely to charge a renewal fee.

Watch out for agents charging you to renew your agreement with a tenant to give you, in theory, two rather than one month's notice. Once a periodic agreement is in place, notice can be served at any time with two months' notice from the landlord and one month from the tenant (the notice period must start from the date the tenancy started).

Ending the tenancy

For advice on how to evict a tenant who has broken the terms of their contract, see pages 160–76. However, most tenancies end happily and the tenant just decides to move on. Nevertheless, this is the point where conflict can develop over any deductions that are made from the deposit, and it is in both your interests to follow the termination process fairly.

- **The tenant should ensure the property** is as clean and tidy as when they moved in.
- **On an agreed date,** check the inventory together (you may ask your agent to do this), checking for damage. If professional cleaning or repairs are necessary, obtain two estimates and show them to the tenant to prove you are handling the matter fairly. Check small details that can end up costing a lot in money or time, such as the vacuum cleaner still has all its attachments, that no fittings have been knocked loose, and that the oven is clean.
- **Check the tenant** has removed all their belongings. If he hasn't, remind him, pointing out that he will be charged for their removal and storage or disposal otherwise.
- **Take meter readings.**
- **The tenant should return all sets of keys.**
- **The tenant should provide a forwarding address.**

If there is a dispute and you are a landlord or tenant, make sure you include the following in your complaint to the deposit scheme:

- **A signed and dated** Tenancy Agreement.
- **The signed and dated** check-in and check-out reports.
- **A collection of signed** and dated photographs.
- **All correspondence** relating to the claim.
- **Each invoice** that relates to the claim.

If you haven't done so already, meet the tenant to discuss and agree any repair bills. This is also a chance for you to get feedback on your property: there may be a noise problem, for example, or the tenant may feel the kitchen fittings have reached the end of their useful life.

'The end of a tenancy is a good time to reassess the property.'

Upgrading

The end of a tenancy is a good time to reassess the property and decide if anything needs replacing or improving. Keep an eye on the local market and see if your competitors are ahead of you in offering, say, broadband access or power showers.

The (hopefully) short period between lets is the ideal time to spruce up the property with some fresh decoration and possibly new furniture. Check how tired the sofa, mattresses and shower curtains are if you are offering a furnished let. You may already know that the kitchen will need updating – kitchens take a real beating when there are a lot of tenants in a house. However, it may be that you only need to change the worktop and, at worst, the doors in the kitchen if you have invested in good solid kitchen units initially. Your upgrade may enable you to charge a higher rent, or stay competitive with local landlords.

Renting a property

Research suggests that more people are considering renting as a long-term option than ever before. This might be due to the costs of buying a home, to survive today's requirement to be 'mobile' for the job market or purely through lifestyle choice.

First decisions

Rental costs are based pretty much on the number of rooms, so it is worth renting the smallest space that meets your needs. Landlords should also read this section to better understand how tenants choose a property.

If you are renting somewhere near work and only need the accommodation during the working week as you will live elsewhere at weekends, you'll probably be better off looking for a room in a house, rather than a more expensive self-contained property. You may also have other priorities, such as security (particularly important in properties that share an entrance) or easy parking.

You'll also need to decide if you want a furnished or unfurnished property. If you are renting with a view to moving into the area, you may want to use your own furniture, as putting it into storage is very expensive. If you are thinking of buying a property in the future, you may be happy to start purchasing items such as beds and wardrobes as you'll need them in your new home and you won't need to go on a shopping spree at that stage. The equipment in furnished flats varies greatly in quality from the stylish and durable to cheap and tacky oddments that the landlord has acquired over the years, probably as cheaply as possible.

'Research the local property market to get a feel for the prices that are charged for what you have in mind.'

With the exponential development of the internet, there has been a huge growth in 'online letting' for finding a property in which to live. To find out more, go to **www.which.co.uk/money/mortgages-and-property**.

'If you rent, you can probably live in an area that you might otherwise not be able to afford.'

What's the market like?

It is worth researching the local market before getting in property details. You will get a feel for the maximum and minimum prices charged for the type of property you are interested in, and whether there are variations according to location. Look at advertisements in local newspapers and have a word with local letting agents (see pages 101–3), asking to see their current rental list. This will also tell you how active the market is and whether demand matches supply – information that may help you negotiate the price down when the time comes. The rental list will also give you an idea of what is coming up in the future, as well as what is available now.

BE CAREFUL!

Check that the rents quoted are weekly or monthly – it makes a big difference! And find out what terms you have to take properties on for, whether it's just for six months, or more.

Where to look

One major plus about renting property is that rents vary less than prices, so you may be able to afford to rent somewhere you can't afford to buy: you can go for the most convenient or pleasing location and see what it costs. Some properties are excellent for renting even if you would not want to buy them. For example, living above a shop can be peaceful and convenient – unless it's one that serves kebabs until two in the morning.

For a private let

To find private property to rent, start your researches with:

- **Local newspaper advertisements,** including *Loot* and *Daltons Weekly*. There are usually plenty of advertisements in newspapers, but attractive properties get snapped up quickly, so get the paper as early as you can and start phoning as soon as office hours commence.
- **Internet sites,** like www.zoopla.co.uk, www.rightmove.co.uk, www.spareroom.co.uk, http://uk.easyroommate.com and many more. As with local newspapers, it takes time for properties to be loaded up to the net, so you still need to contact letting agents directly.
- **Advertisements in post offices and other shops.** These are an excellent source of local information, which is particularly good if you already live where you want to rent.

This cheap form of marketing is very popular with small-scale landlords who have one or two rooms to let.

- **Work.** Human resources departments may be able to advise on local accommodation, and there may be a noticeboard with advertisements. It isn't always easy living and working in the same place, so try to make sure that you really do get on with the person you are looking to rent with.
- **Talking to friends and contacts** is useful if they can recommend a good landlord or warn you off a dodgy one. You may find out which properties are likely to be available before they hit the high street, so you can get in early.
- **Letting agents.** All the above search methods can be time consuming, and you might find it easier to let an agent do the work and provide you with a list of suitable properties. Usually they produce a free list on a daily/weekly basis, or some agents will charge an arrangement fee for finding a specific property, which is usually somewhere between £25 and £150. For advice on choosing a letting agent, see pages 101–3.
- **Accommodation agencies.** If you are a student, start with the university accommodation office for information and advice, and then perhaps tour the local accommodation agencies because they work in this market sector. For more information on accommodation agencies, see page 103.

For social tenancies

Local councils usually allocate their accommodation on a points system or a banding system in which priority is given to people who have lived in the area for a certain length of time but other factors relating to specific needs are also considered. Your council should be able to provide a leaflet explaining how their system works. There is often a long waiting list.

You could also try a **housing association**, also sometimes known as **registered providers of social housing**. These are non-profit-making bodies that aim to provide affordable accommodation and are one of the major providers of state-funded housing. In many cases they have taken over what was council housing stock. There is a central waiting list for all council and housing association homes in most areas, but some housing associations also run their own separate waiting lists.

If you have a postcode of the area you are in, **www.gov.uk** will give you information on the local council and also provide a link to their website.

Key questions to ask yourself

What are my needs? Do they include:

- Number of rooms, especially bedrooms, and whether they need to be double or single?
- Parking space required?
- Furnished or unfurnished?
- Close to local transport or shops?
- Storage space?
- Telephone points (including broadband)?

Add to this your preferences:

- Bath or shower?
- Do you want an open-plan kitchen?
- Do you want a garden?

Other questions worth considering are:

- Would you be prepared to share the accommodation, or part of it, with other people?
- Would you share with a live-in landlord?
- Do you want or need to be on the ground floor?
- Do you feel you will have enough privacy?
- Will you be sharing with anyone else? If so, meet them to see how you get on.

Have you got children or pets?

If you have children or pets you obviously need space for them, including a garden, and will want to know the accommodation is suitable and safe for them. Some landlords will let to tenants with children or pets, but they are few and far between, so start looking in plenty of time before you need to rent somewhere. Check the place before you view and the contract terms and conditions. Visit www.letswithpets.org.uk for more help.

What to look for

The most important question is what can you afford? Most rents are charged by the calendar month and you will pay utility bills and Council Tax on top of this. Look through your last three months' bank statements and work out what you can afford to pay from your income.

Also consider how long you are likely to want the accommodation for (most lets are for a fixed term of six months that is renewable), and whether you are likely to want to extend this. Some lets are short-term only, and there may be a definite ending time if, for example, the owner is working abroad for a set period.

Location

As always with property, location is the key. If you prefer to use public transport, you need to be near a train or bus route. You may want to live near family, friends, work or a certain school, or like the look of an area. However, as when buying a property, do visit at least twice, at different times of day, to investigate noise levels and traffic conditions, or neighbours! Work out practicalities, such as where you will do grocery shopping and how safe you feel on your route to the bus stop, college or your work.

What do you need?

You need to be clear about what you need. For example, it is not worth renting a property with a spare room if it is not going to be used frequently: it is cheaper to put guests (or yourself!) up in a local hotel or B & B for the night, or buy a sofa bed. Quality, size and price vary enormously. Write a list of your needs, such as those listed on page 95.

BE CAREFUL!

When you phone to check the property is still available, get as much information as possible to save wasted visits. Take basic safety precautions, such as telling someone else where you are going. Get the landline and mobile number of the person you are meeting. If possible, go along with someone else for security and a second opinion.

'Most lets are for a six-month term that is renewable, but others are short term. Check that the property you want to rent has an appropriate letting period for what you are looking for.'

The cost of renting

The nearer a city centre and the more luxurious the property, the higher the price will be. Suburban and rural properties tend to be cheaper per room – but your transport costs are likely to be higher.

It can be tricky assessing the merits of prices between properties because you are not necessarily comparing like with like. To make an assessment of the value for money (as opposed to aesthetic considerations, such as the décor or how nice the view is), try the following process:

- **Make sure you are comparing** the price per calendar month (pcm). Charges per week will seem lower when multiplied by four but this is not the monthly charge, as most months are longer than 28 days. If the price given is per week, multiply it by 52 and divide by 12 for a true monthly comparison.
- **Consider the price per room.**
- **Calculate the price per square foot.** The agent or landlord should be able to tell you the area of the accommodation and it should have been calculated as part of the Energy Performance Certificate. Divide this number into the monthly rent to find the cost per square foot. This allows you to make a rational comparison of how much space you are getting for your money. For example, a one-bedroom flat covering 100 sq m and costing £569 per month costs £5.69 per sq m (569 divided by 100 = £5.69). The cost for a two-bedroom flat the same size with a monthly rent of £704 would be £7.04 per sq m (704 divided by 100). Obviously this would become more attractive if two tenants shared the rent.
- **Consider other factors,** such as location, fittings, furnishings and décor. Obviously the better these are, the higher the premium.
- **Take into account terms and conditions,** such as how much deposit is required, and particularly what bills are included – or are they extra?

As a guideline, the table overleaf shows some average cost of accommodation per calendar

> **'When comparing prices, make sure you are comparing like for like.'**

Average cost of accommodation per calendar month (2012)

How the average cost of renting in inner London compares with the rest of Great Britain.

	1-bed flat	2-bed flat	2-bed terrace	3-bed semi-detached	4-bed detached
London	**£1,275**	**£1,700**	**£1,800**	**£2,300**	**£3,250**
Great Britain	**£570**	**£700**	**£740**	**£800**	**£1,300**

Other costs to be aware of

There are other costs to take into account:

Deposit (returnable)	equivalent of 4–6 weeks' rent
EITHER: Reservation deposit	up to £200 or the equivalent of the first month's rent, usually refundable
OR: Administration fee	£100 plus
Tenancy reference	£50 plus
Agreement fee	£25
Inventory fee	£75–£150
Renewal fee	£150 plus

Jargon buster

Deposit A sum of money that is paid in advance to cover any potential costs of damage to the rented property or should you fail to pay the rent. If there is no damage when you leave the property, all the deposit should be returned to you.
Guarantor Someone, often a parent, who agrees to pay the rent for the tenant in case of default.
Inventory A list of items that are in the rented property on your arrival.
Reservation fee A sum of money that may be payable to a letting agency to keep a property on hold while you get hold of a deposit and/or your references.

month. The table illustrates that prices in London are more than double the average for the rest of Great Britain.

Not all letting agents charge fees, and they vary from firm to firm, so it shop around and find the right letting agent for the type of property you want and fees that seem to be fair.

Cheques and references

Some landlords and agencies won't accept personal cheques as deposits or rent in advance, so you might have to pay in cash or organise a banker's draft.

There are different types of tenant agreements, although most of them are what is called an 'assured shorthold tenancy', which gives the landlord more rights than an 'assured tenancy'. The chapter Tenancy Law on pages 127–48 explains further.

BE CAREFUL!
If you are paying your rent weekly, the landlord must provide you with a rent book, which is filled in each week.

- **When paying cash,** get another person to go with you and always ask for a written receipt.
- **Some landlords want rent** to be paid by standing order so you may need a bank account.
- **You may also be asked to provide a reference:** bank details or a letter from your employer confirming your employment are usually sufficient, but you may be asked for a character reference or a reference from a previous landlord. It will save time if you arrange these in advance and take copies with you when you view. For first-time tenants a letter from a parent or guardian should be enough.
- **Some landlords ask for a guarantor** to pay the rent if you don't (see pages 30 and 200). Check what the guarantor is agreeing to: in some cases they are held to be liable for costs, which include rent owed, damage to the property and any costs of evicting you, the tenant, from the property.

Whatever you are renting, find out why the property or room is available, it will give you an idea of how long the property might be yours for, or if there is a set time. The longer you agree to rent a property for, the better rate you may be able to negotiate.

What the tenant pays for

One of the critical things that you need to understand is what charges you will be responsible for. For short-term lets, these are often included in the rent, whereas for longer-term rents, you are likely to have to pay for:

- Electricity, gas and water.
- Council Tax.
- TV licence.
- Telephone.
- Any broadband charges.

Make sure that these bills are either in your name, or, if renting with others, in everyone's name as then the responsibility is spread, just in case someone decides not to pay. Be careful not to tie yourself into too long a contract bearing in mind most contracts are initially for six months. Ask if you can take the contract with you if you should move. If you leave, make sure you check the readings and advise and obtain acceptance letters of the day you are moving out. Most utility companies will accept about ten days' notice for change of address.

If you are taking on these bills, make sure you see how much it costs and if you can reduce the monthly price by paying by direct debit – or indeed changing the supplier. Note that you will also be responsible for the insurance cover on your own possessions (see pages 75–6).

Letting agents and landlords

A good letting agent will find you a suitable property, negotiate the tenancy, and only charge you when you pick up the keys. It can be well worth the money for the saved hassle, time and foot slog.

A dodgy letting agent might find you decent accommodation, but they'll charge (and overcharge) for minor administrative tasks and get you to sign agreements with small print that commits you to pay them for doing almost anything except blowing your nose. You don't have to use a letting agent to find property (see the list of other routes on pages 93–4), but your choice may be restricted if you do not.

The property letting market is unregulated and it is growing fast, creating conditions where there are many opportunities for unscrupulous agents to make a quick buck. They can do this because people looking for accommodation are often in a hurry and are understandably keener to discuss the size of the kitchen and how many bedrooms a property has than whether they will be expected to pay for repairing rotten windows or to be charged £30 for letters telling them the rent is going up.

There are about 17,000 letting agents in the UK. About 8,000 are members of trade bodies (see box, left) and if at all possible you should stick with them because then you'll have some comeback if there's a dispute, as they will have a code of conduct that they have to stick to. It is wise to check if a firm is a member of one of these bodies (it's easy to do this through their websites) rather than just take their word for it.

Letting trade bodies

Sadly the Government continues to shy away from regulating letting agents, so choose ones that offer you and your money some protection. The best protection on offer are at:

- The National Approved Letting Scheme (NALS): www.nalscheme.co.uk
- The Association of Residential Letting Agents (ARLA): www.arla.co.uk
- The Property Ombudsman: www.tpos.co.uk
- The Royal Institution of Chartered Surveyors (RICS): www.rics.org
- Safe Agents: www.safeagents.co.uk.

A letting and management service is also sometimes offered by these bodies. Each runs its own code of practice, but NALS and The Property Ombudsman offer further security with an internal complaints procedure, a legally binding arbitration service and a scheme to protect money if it is lost or misappropriated.

Finding a letting agent

There are different types of letting agency that you can use:

- **Some find tenants for properties** and are also known as accommodation agencies (see page 103).
- **Others manage the property as well** so the tenant deals with them, rather than the landlord.
- **Many estate agents** offer a lettings service as well as selling property, so they may belong to several of the schemes in the box, opposite.

Legally, agents represent landlords but they can charge fees to both landlords and tenants. Some don't charge tenants at all, but others have fees for drawing up tenancy agreements, providing inventories and administrative costs, such as phone calls and postage.

Letting agents advertise in local papers and there is also often a list in housing advice offices and local bureaux of Citizens Advice (www.adviceguide.org.uk). Because registration is free, it makes sense to sign up with any that you feel you can trust (see box, on page 100). They'll ask you about your needs (see page 95) and how much you want to pay. If they supply details of suitable properties, follow it up straightaway as good accommodation gets snapped up quickly. They may invite you to contact the landlord or, if they are offering a fuller service, show you round it themselves.

Once you decide to rent a property, the agency may ask for a holding deposit to remove the property from the market while they take up your references – another reason to take copies of references with you when viewing. This is not the same as a deposit on the tenancy, and you could lose it if you pull out of the rental process.

BE CAREFUL!

It is against the law for a letting agent to charge a registration fee for property details: if you are asked to do this, head straight for the door.

Identifying a good agent

The best recommendation is word of mouth, so ask friends and local contacts if they know an agent with a good record. They will be members of a recognised trade association (see box, opposite) or at least follow the NALS scheme or are ARLA registered: look for the logo, and ask if they are still members. Check the local paper and relevant website (some firms fraudulently claim to be members, or have left but still display its signage). These websites are also good for finding agents in the area if you lack local information.

Some agents don't charge tenants at all. Others do, which is quite reasonable given the amount of work involved in managing a rented property well, but good agents

BE CAREFUL!

Although you pay a fee to an agent, their main income is from their client, the landlord, so bear in mind they are likely to give the landlord's needs more priority than yours. That also means that the legal agreement is likely to be in the landlord's favour, so make sure you get an independent person to check any legal documents before you sign.

will tell you early on what you are expected to pay for and will provide a receipt for it. Ask for a list of likely charges when you first meet them; see the box on page 98 for a list of likely costs.

Sign up with as many reputable agents as you can (this is free) and continue to look for accommodation by other routes as suggested on pages 93–4, as many are still likely to be cheaper than going through an agent. You will then cover all possibilities and are less likely to miss out on a good property at a reasonable rent.

Unfair fees

Some letting agents sneak all sorts of extra charges into their contracts, so it is really important to read the small print before you sign an agreement with them. Don't just sign up in the office without reading the document, however desperate you are for accommodation. Ask for a copy in advance, or take it away with you. Examples of unfair fees used by some unscrupulous agents include the following:

- A fee for information on rental properties
- A charge for sending letters, even ones telling you the rent is going up
- A penalty payment if you don't pay the rent by standing order
- A charge for moving out as well as one for moving in
- A charge for re-let even when the landlord agrees to re-let the property early.

Spotting a bad agent

Naturally your mind will be focused on the accommodation you want, not spotting deficiencies in the agency. However, there are things to watch out for that could save you money and hassle. A letting agent who is unprofessional in their dealings with you is likely to be just as unfair with the landlord, which is a recipe for disaster. Here are some indicators that an agent could be dodgy.

- **Not a member** of one of the trade associations listed on page 100.
- **Poorly organised,** so you always get the answerphone, the office is untidy, and they miss appointments.

Are you receiving benefits or credits?

As your benefits are typically paid in arrears, you will have to find the first month's rent and the deposit yourself, although some local authorities or charities may have ways to support you with a loan. Not all landlords can accept tenants on benefits, possibly because they can't get the insurance to cover the let or they are restricted by their mortgage lender.

- **Asks for money up front.**
- **Doesn't offer receipts.**
- **Doesn't give you time** to check agreements.
- **Doesn't do an inventory.**
- **Doesn't explain arrangements** clearly.
- **Include a plethora of financial penalties** in tenancy agreements.

Accommodation agencies

These are more specialised letting agents and if you are a student, you are more likely to come across them. They charge tenants who take up accommodation a small fee (typically a week or two's rent, but sometimes less – and see Unfair fees, opposite). Some student accommodation offices allow you to search for property online, which is very useful if you do not yet live in the area.

They tend not to be able to offer services, such as showing you round the property: rather they are a contact point between student and landlord. If you are interested in a property, you'll probably be asked for a holding deposit, which you would lose if you change your mind. Finally, demand can outstrip supply in this market: if this is the case in your local market, you may need to start your search early to find rooms for the new academic year. In others, you will have more choice and can take your time.

BE CAREFUL!

Under the Accommodation Agencies Act of 1953, an agency cannot charge for registering your details and/or supplying addresses. However, some agencies try to do this, dressing them up as registration or administration fees. If they try this, walk away: the only payment they are entitled to is for providing details of accommodation that you subsequently rent. You can safely register with as many agencies as you like at no cost.

Finding a landlord

There are several ways to locate landlords apart from relying on who is advertising at the moment. There are two trade bodies, the NLA and the RLA (see box, page 100), and local councils, colleges and landlords associations run accreditation schemes that set minimum requirements for landlords. Details on this can be found from Accreditation Network UK (ANUK) (see overleaf). Ask the landlord to show you their accreditation scheme membership card or certificate. The landlord is responsible for:

- **Repairs and maintenance** to the structure and exterior.
- **All sanitary installations.**

University websites have links to their accommodation office Also try **www.accommodationforstudents.com**, **www.homesforstudents.co.uk** and **www.studentaccommodation.org**. There is more advice available from **www.shelter.org.uk** and **www.propertychecklists.co.uk**.

- **Heating and hot water** installations.
- **The safety of gas, electrics and electrical appliances** (see page 53).
- **The fire safety of furniture and furnishings** supplied by the landlord.
- **In a flat or maisonette,** other parts of the building the landlord owns or controls and whose condition would affect the tenant.
- **Complying with the legal regulations** of owning and letting out a property.

The landlord can claim against any tenants who cause damage to their property.

Avoid rogue landlords/letting agents!

Many people complain about being badly treated by landlords/agents. If you ask these three questions, though, you can avoid most rogue ones.

1. Will my deposit be protected in a tenancy deposit protection scheme? If yes, which one?
2. Can you bring a copy of a current gas and electrical safety certificate with you on visits?
3. Can I have a copy of the EPC (see page 54)?

If a landlord or letting agent says no or can't provide any of these, walk away.

Meeting a landlord

For your own security, always get a landline phone number as well as any mobile numbers offered, plus an address. The landlord is likely to ask you for references and it is reasonable for you to do the same: is he a member of a trade body such as the NLA or RLA? Can he supply contact details of other tenants who can vouch for him? If possible, visit other properties let by the landlord (he may have several in the same block or nearby).

The encounter won't necessarily feel very comfortable: after all, you are both in the process of checking the other one out, and the landlord will want to make sure his new tenant is going to look after the property, which he may have sunk his life savings into buying. The landlord will probably also have been through this process many times before, so his responses may be trotted out quite fast.

As with agents, be suspicious of anybody who appears disorganised or unforthcoming with information. Do not pay any money before checking the contract. This person will have access to your temporary home, and you need to feel you can trust them. Ask your local Citizens Advice Bureau, Shelter or other housing advice office if any landlords in the area have caused concern in the past.

Some useful contacts are: the National Landlord's Association (NLA) (**www.landlords. org.uk**); the Residential Landlords Association (RLA) (**www.rla.org.uk**) and the Accreditation Network UK (**www.anuk.org.uk**).

Viewing a property

If at all possible, you should view a property at least twice to get a feel for what it is like to live in it and its surrounding area. After all, you might end up spending longer living there than a person who purchased the property next door.

Always view properties during daylight hours as that is when flaws show up best. Follow the suggested list of vital checks that follows on this page and on page 107 and also bear in mind the 'key questions' given on page 106.

Vital checks

Make a list of the priorities of what you want from the property and score each one as you view properties to help you come to a decision.

If you will be sharing the tenancy, agree this list in advance, and if at all possible, view the potential properties together.

- **Study the exterior** and judge if it is well maintained. If the outside is badly maintained, the interior is likely to be in a poor state of repair, too. Are the windows in good condition? Do the gutters leak? The landlord or agent won't tell you if the neighbours are noisy, but the current tenants might if you get a chance to talk to them, or you may know someone who lives in the road and so be able to check with them directly.
- **When you get inside,** do check that lights work, taps produce water and windows open. Every property has its own atmosphere and you get a gut feeling for places you feel comfortable

'The exterior of a rented property is just as important as the interior. A well-maintained building shows that the landlord cares about it.'

A landlord has legal responsibilities, ranging from fire safety and smoke alarms to various types of insurance. If you want to find out more, see the advice for landlords given on pages 74-7.

Key questions to ask the landlord

Key questions to ask when you are interested in renting a property include:

- Why is the property or room available?
- What is the rent (as a monthly or weekly figure)?
- Does the rent include any costs such as water and electricity?
- Is a deposit required? And, if so, how much is it and which company is it protected by?
- When is the property available from and to?
- How much notice do I need to give to leave? How should this notice be given?
- What Council Tax is payable?
- How is the property heated (even if you're viewing in the summer!)?
- How much are the heating and electricity bills?
- If I'm responsible for their payment, can I change the supplier if I choose?
- Can I please see the EPC and Gas and Electrical Safety Certificate?
- Who do I contact if repairs are necessary? (This must be a UK address.)
- Are there any special clauses in the contract that I should be told about?
- Are children and/or pets allowed (if relevant)?

Is the rent reasonable?

Draw on the research you did at the start of the process to answer the question 'Is this property worth the rent being asked?' If it isn't, you may be able to negotiate the price down and you stand a better chance of success if you can explain why your price is more reasonable than theirs. Before you agree to rent a property, double check that you can afford it, factoring in the estimated amounts for utilities, Council Tax and other bills.

in. Unlike a buyer, you won't be able to change the décor or, if provided, furnishings. If you hate them, don't condemn yourself to the torture of living with them. If, however, you are renting for a while, the landlord may be OK with you changing it. It's always worth asking!

- **If the property you're looking at was built after June 1992,** it must have smoke alarms on every floor. All electrical equipment must be safe to use, including the power sockets.
- **If the property is occupied,** check to see if the tenants are using extension cables to run appliances, which would suggest there are not enough sockets for everyday use.
- **Any property rented out** should have a gas and electric safety certificate and all furnishings must meet the fire safety regulations (see page 74–5).
- **An Energy Performance Certificate** (see page 54) should also be supplied for all properties marketed for rent.

If at all possible, ask if you can view the property again at another time of day. This will allow you to check for noise levels, see how much light enters the rooms. Visiting during rush hour allows you to judge traffic noise and ease of parking. Even if you can't get in, you can get a fair idea of this from outside the property. In the meantime, ask for a copy of an example tenancy agreement.

Safety first

You should be given a copy of the official safety record for the furniture, furnishings, gas appliances and recent electrical work.

- Furniture and furnishings must meet fire safety regulations unless they were made before 1950.
- The gas appliances and supply should be checked once a year by someone on the Gas Safety Register. There should be a record of inspection dates, defects identified and action taken.
- Although there is no legal requirement for landlords to install carbon monoxide detectors, it is worth asking about this valuable safety equipment. The detectors are available from hardware stores.

'Every property has its own atmosphere and you get a gut feeling for places that you feel comfortable in.'

Entering into a contract

As well as understanding the contract, ensure the deposit, inventory and insurance are handled well. The deposit and inventory, in particular, are the most frequent areas of disagreement, but this need not necessarily be the case.

The contract

Never sign a contract without reading and understanding it, however desperate you are to get hold of the keys to the property.

There is advice on all aspects of contracts on pages 79–82, 128–34 and 190–204.

Safety first

- A deposit is largely defined as any money that is held in any way, shape or form to guarantee the tenant abides by the agreement, then any monies that are over and above normal rent payments can be considered as a deposit.
- Even before you have a written agreement, any verbal understanding counts as a legal agreement - although they are harder to enforce. It is in both your interests to understand your rights and responsibilities. Get anything you agree in writing.
- Always view a deposit in person and meet the agent or the landlord at the property first. Have a handover meeting at the property on move-in day and never hand over a deposit to a company or landlord purely on the basis of an internet advert.

The deposit

You will be asked to pay a deposit to cover any damage you cause to the property and as insurance in case you default on the rent. The deposit is usually based on the value of 4–6 weeks' rent. This is perfectly fair, but getting the deposit back after moving out of a rented property often causes more problems than any other aspect of renting property. Here are some ways that you can help yourself:

- **Make a dated note** if any items are removed from the property by the landlord or agent in order to avoid misunderstandings at a later date about where they have got to.
- **Make sure you get a receipt** for the deposit.

Since April 2007 in England and Wales and in 2012 in Scotland, legislation (the tenancy deposit scheme) has come into effect to help overcome the conflict that surrounds the subject of deposits (see pages 60–2 for more information).

Since April 2007 and 2012, there are strict rules for where landlords bank deposit money – for more information, see page 83.

If you are paying your deposit by cheque, you'll have to wait until it clears before you can move in. If it is urgent, you could pay with a banker's draft, a building society cheque or cash. The simplest way to ensure you pay the rent on time is to set up a standing order. Landlords do not take kindly to late payment. See also the advice on guarantors on page 84.

At the end of the tenancy, do not withhold the last month's rent on the assumption that the deposit more than covers the amount: the landlord or their agent will want to assess the state of the property at the end of the let, so cannot make deductions from the deposit before then.

The inventory

It is in your and the landlord's interest to make a full inventory of what is in the property (see pages 85–6). This is a list of everything you could be held responsible for damaging or losing, including furniture and other items such as kitchen equipment. It is by far the best option to be present when the landlord or agent makes this list, as you can agree on what is present. Be thorough about this. For example, look at the carpet under beds and sofas to see if they are stained: you do not want to be held responsible for damage that is already there.

If you cannot be present at the inspection, or are simply issued with a list, check it thoroughly with another person and get them to witness it. If something is missing or damaged, inform the landlord in writing immediately. Take photographs of any damage present before you began living there, and date them. If no one provides you with an inventory (a major warning sign of a dodgy landlord), make one yourself, take a copy, and send it to the landlord together with any photographs, if relevant. You should also consider why a landlord would not undertake this basic procedure and keep a careful eye on his dealings during your residency.

If anything is removed during your tenure, make a dated note

BE CAREFUL!

While there are plenty of stories of landlords from hell, there are many of tenants who have behaved irresponsibly too. You might want a reference from your landlord in the future or need to negotiate with her: if you've been fair with them, they are more likely to be fair with you.

You can find more advice on making or getting an independent inventory at **www.theaiic.co.uk**. There is more information on contracts, the deposit and inventory on pages 79–87.

and, if possible, take a photograph. Evidence could be invaluable if there is a dispute about items in the property in the future.

If you can, repair any damage you have caused, or replace items that cannot be made good. If you can't do this, you must expect to be charged for repairs. Make sure the property is clean at the end of the let – you could have the carpets professionally cleaned or hire a carpet cleaner and your contract may require you to do this anyway. Take photographs of the property on the day you leave, showing its condition (this is most useful if you photographed any damaged items at the start of the tenancy).

If the inventory is carried out by the letting agent, there is usually a charge (see page 87). Typically the landlord and tenant share the cost – one paying for moving in and one moving out – but better agents and landlords don't charge the tenants at all. If you are paying a high deposit, it may be worth investing in an independent inventory if the letting agent or landlord are not intending to do so.

Insurance

While you are listing the items in the inventory, make a separate list of your own possessions, if you have not done so already. This will help you decide the value of the insurance cover you should now take out. To ease any claims you may have to make, ensure you have photos of costly items, any serial numbers on equipment and always keep your receipts somewhere safe. The landlord's insurance policy only covers the buildings and his possessions. Sadly, rented properties are often targeted by burglars, especially in areas where students live, as they know there are likely to be portable and valuable items such as hi-fis and computers in many of the rooms. Some insurance brokers have special policies for people who rent rooms or whole properties.

Policies in high-risk inner city postcodes sometimes carry a requirement to have minimum-security locks on doors and accessible windows/locks, which may require negotiation with the landlord. If you are in social housing, your local authority may run an insurance scheme for the tenants. As always with insurance, it pays to shop around, provided you are confident you are comparing like with like.

Policies can be bedroom-rated (based on the number of bedrooms) or sum-insured (based on the cost of your belongings) and it is worth getting quotes based on both methods.

Companies who specialise in flat-share insurance include Endsleigh (**www.endsleigh. co.uk**), Entertainment and Leisure Insurance (**www.eandl.co.uk**), Harrison Beaumont (**www.hbinsurance.co.uk**) and Leisure Insure (**www.leisureinsure.co.uk**).

A tenant's obligations

It's worth being a good tenant because you might want to rent from the landlord or agent again, or need a reference from them.

Although being a tenant does not carry the responsibilities of home ownership (which is one of its joys), it does come with certain expectations of behaviour and basic maintenance. As a tenant you are also expected to:

- **Pay your rent on time,** usually a month in advance.
- **Live in the property** and not leave it empty. If you go on holiday, tell your landlord. Otherwise they might think you have left and are trying to avoid paying rent. Also an inhabited property is less likely to be burgled than one that is standing empty.
- **Keep the property secure,** which means locking doors and, if possible, windows when you go out and not giving the keys to non-tenants.
- **Have a general responsibility** to look after the property reasonably and inform the landlord of any repairs required. A good landlord will appreciate being told of such maintenance needs as promptly as possible, because it could prevent a worse problem developing and it is likely to be a condition of your tenancy agreement. For example, a leaking pipe left to drip could damage flooring or bring down a neighbour's ceiling. Minor maintenance such as replacing light bulbs is down to you.
- **Undertake basic maintenance,** such as changing light bulbs, tightening loose screws and replacing smoke alarm batteries. If you need to contact the landlord, try to do so at sociable hours unless it is a genuine emergency.
- **Respect your neighbours** by keeping the place reasonably tidy, clearing rubbish, not playing loud music late at night. That doesn't mean you have to

'Look after the property reasonably and tell your landlord of any necessary repairs as soon as possible.'

Moving in

- Before you physically move in make sure you have checked the inventory.
- Read and make sure you understand the contract before moving in.
- Check you have been given a copy of the gas safety certificate.
- Know where any fire exits are, and check you can get to them.
- Contact the utility companies and take meter readings on the day you move in.
- Set up your standing order so that the rent is paid on time. Keep track of your finances so that you know you can afford to pay the rent (sometimes bills can be higher than you thought, or unexpected events affect your finances).

'Always try to be professional in your dealings with the landlord.'

live like a monk, but anti-social behaviour can be grounds for eviction. Remember that you can also be held responsible for the behaviour of guests.

- **Use it as a home,** not a base for a business, unless agreed with the landlord/agency.

Be professional in your dealings with the landlord or agent. They are running the property as a business and you are their client. Make notes of conversations where appropriate (for example, if the landlord says he'll fix a broken toilet before the weekend) and confirm any important details in writing. Keep a copy of all communications, including emails and notes of telephone calls. If you are sharing the property, it makes sense to keep all this paperwork in one well-organised file so that everybody knows what is going on. Include all contact details in the file so that everyone has access to them. Treat

Tips for a trouble-free tenancy

- Read, understand and follow the terms of the tenancy. If the landlord does not do the same, point this out politely.
- Pay the rent on time.
- Pay other bills on time.
- Communicate promptly when necessary.
- Ask permission if you want to do things such as sublet, take in a lodger, pass the tenancy to someone else, or make improvements to the property.
- Treat the property with respect.
- Try not to antagonise the neighbours - if you are having a party, tell them (you don't have to invite them!).
- End the tenancy properly (see pages 89-90).

BE CAREFUL!
Beware of being charged a renewal fee by a letting agent: they are employed by the landlord, not you, and you should not have to make any payments that are not specified in your original agreement.

the tenancy as a job of work that you need to stay on top of.

Don't let yourself be treated as if you are some kind of paying guest: for the duration of your tenancy this is your home where you have a right to feel safe and happy. Some landlords can be over-zealous in their understandable wish to protect their property, but all have to give you a right to enjoy the property quietly and an amount of notice if they want access to the property. That said, if you annoy the neighbours, they are likely to complain to the landlord, who is likely to want to keep relations amicable: he'll probably know the neighbours for longer than he'll have contact with you.

Sharing a house with others

Living with other people, especially if they are strangers and/or you are sharing communal areas, isn't always easy. To help make the tenancy work out well, follow this advice.

- **Try to meet all the tenants** before you move in, and find out what the other people do for a living (early or late working patterns will mean people entering and leaving at unsocial hours, for example). Ask if they tend to socialise together or lead separate lives.
- **Agree how bills will be shared out.** It clearly makes sense to divide Council Tax and utility bills by the number of people sharing, but if one person uses significantly more of one utility than the others – perhaps by excessive use of an electric heater – there is likely to be conflict.
- **Establish what the agreed system is for paying shared bills** and cleaning communal areas. If there aren't any house rules, there is a lot of scope for conflict so perhaps you could suggest some. House rules should be in writing and include:
  - Agreeing which parts of the property are communal, and which rooms no one can enter without permission.
  - A cleaning rota.
  - Is smoking allowed, and if so, where in the property?
  - Can tenants have guests to stay over regularly?

For more information on letting agents, see pages 68–71. Although much of that information is aimed at the landlord, there is useful advice there that applies just as well to the tenant. For help moving all your addresses, visit **www.iammoving.com**.

Disputes

Most disputes begin with small incidents that could have been avoided with decent communication, and then the problem escalates. It is easy to feel vulnerable when you are a tenant. A landlord or their representative who is responsible for unpleasant or abusive phone calls, unexpected visits, interference in the supply of utilities or other forms of intimidation, which make your life at home difficult, may well be guilty of harassment, which is a criminal offence.

Can I come in?

One frequent source of conflict is whether the landlord has the right to enter the premises. There are some who seem to think they can pop in and use the toilet if they happen to be passing! The tenancy agreement should include an explanation of how and when your landlord has access to the property. You are entitled to reasonable notice of this (usually 24 or 48 hours, preferably in writing), except in emergencies such as a flooded kitchen.

Who can help?

You may be able to get advice from:

- A tenancy relations officer or specialist in harassment issues in the local housing or environmental health departments.
- A housing aid centre.
- Citizens Advice (www.adviceguide.org.uk).
- Shelter (www.shelter.org.uk).
- A law centre.
- A solicitor.

'Harassment from a landlord or his or her representative can be intimidating and most unpleasant. It is a criminal offence and, as such, you have rights for dealing with it.'

The accredited tenant scheme

Landlords who are members of an accredited landlord scheme (see box, page 104) should know if it includes an accredited tenant scheme. These recognise good tenants and provide a reference that is useful when moving within the rented sector or as a general character reference.

If you are involved in a dispute with your landlord, get advice early as someone may be able to intervene and mediate. If all else fails, see pages 160–73 for dealing with legal action. Pages 174–6 specifically covers harassment from a landlord.

Money matters

6

This chapter looks at small-scale and larger-scale letting businesses. Among other things, it describes how to keep on top of records and how to calculate your profit and pay your tax. The benefits of setting up a limited company and planning for capital gains are also looked at.

Rent as 'extra income'

Earnings from rent are counted as income, so you will have to pay tax on the profit you make on it. This section looks at all the paperwork, tax and legal information you will need to come to grips with early on.

Before becoming a landlord, it is important to have a clear understanding of how the system works, and how much you are likely to be liable to have to pay to Her Majesty's Revenue & Customs (HMRC): it might change how you do things, or whether you decide it is worth letting property at all.

Keeping records

Profit is what is left once you have deducted the allowable expenses from the rental income, which will be mainly rent. Other sums you may receive that count as income include a charge for use of furniture, or for cleaning or providing heat. It is taxed at the same rates as income from business or employment, 20–50 per cent in 2013 and 20–45 per cent in 2013/14, depending on the income band you fall into. If you let more than one property, the income is grouped so you can offset a loss on one property against a profit from another.

Deductible (or 'allowable') expenses

The expenses you can deduct from letting income include:

- Letting agent fees.
- Legal fees for lets of a year or less, or for renewing a lease for less than 50 years.
- Accountancy fees.
- Insurance.
- Interest on property loans.
- Maintenance and repairs (but not improvements).
- Utility bills if you are responsible for them.
- Ground rent and service charges.
- Council Tax.
- Services you pay for, such as cleaning or gardening.
- Other costs of letting the property, such as advertising, phone calls, and travel to and from it.
- Professional fees, such as belonging to a landlord's association.
- Energy performance certificates.
- Tenancy deposit protection.
- Legal fees (for advice on letting issues, but not for buying or selling the property or for planning applications).
- Bad debts.
- Capital allowances for office equipment involved in running the business (see page 118).

You can only deduct expenses that are directly related to letting the property. If the expense is partly for another business, or if you use the property yourself, you can only claim for part of it. For example, if you go to a town and stay overnight partly for leisure, partly for business, you can only claim a proportion of the expense, not all.

What you can't claim

You can't deduct:

- Capital costs, such as the property itself, or the furniture.
- Personal expenses unrelated to your business.
- Any loss from selling the property.

Go to the experts

Property tax is incredibly complex and it is difficult to generalise as it is bespoke to your – and your family's – individual circumstances.

It is therefore essential that you seek advice from a property tax specialist as well as check any advice with HMRC before you even think about buying a property, let alone start receiving rent. With buy to let you are likely to be classed as a 'property investor' – someone who invests in property for ongoing income. Professional advice can cost around £200 per hour, which may seem a lot of money, but it can save you thousands.

When considering what tax you will pay, you need to take into consideration your earnings. Think, too, about what your reasons are for investing in buy to let; for example, is it to boost your pension or pass capital on to your children? A specialist tax adviser will need to know your intentions right from the outset so that he or she can advise you how best to invest your money and to help you know the tax implications and when you will be billed.

Top tips to make your tax returns easier include:

- **Seek help from a tax specialist,** at least in your first year.
- **Keep your records for six years** after the tax year to which they apply.
- **Don't forget to sign and date your tax return** – it's one of the most common mistakes.
- **Speak to the tax office** if you have any queries.

BE CAREFUL!

If you are using the Rent-a-Room Scheme (see page 120), the tax rules are different, so discuss this with your financial adviser.

For more information on running a small business and the associated tax implications, go to the HMRC website: **www.hmrc.gov.uk**, and also **www.gov.uk**, where there are leaflets and booklets to help you.

- **Keep up to date with changes to tax** via a landlord association, your property tax specialist, or specialist landlord magazines.

Capital cost allowances

Capital costs are expenditure on assets, such as the property itself, furniture and machinery. You can claim for some of these. A distinction is made between repairs (fixing or replacing a leaking gutter), which are running costs and therefore deductible, and improvements (refurbishing a kitchen), which are capital expenditure. Replacing traditional materials with modern ones is usually classified as a repair: so, for example, you can replace a single-glazed wooden window frame with a double-glazed PVC sealed unit and set the cost against tax.

Other examples of capital costs you can claim include: office, cleaning and gardening equipment, or a boiler.

Furnishings and equipment

You have a choice on how you claim for furnishings and equipment including small items like cutlery: either 'wear and tear' or 'cost and replacement'. 'Wear and tear' is 10 per cent of the rent less amounts paid by the landlord, which would usually be paid by the tenant (such as Council Tax). See the table, below, for a typical calculation. You can't claim 'wear and tear' on furnished holiday lettings in the UK (see opposite).

BE CAREFUL!

Once you've chosen which of these allowances to claim, you can't switch between them from year to year.

Get the Green Deal

The Government is keen to encourage homeowners to make their properties as energy efficient as possible. From January 2013, there is £125 million available as a cashback offer to improve homes. From April 2016 this will mean that, as a landlord, you won't be able to 'unreasonably' refuse a tenant's request for energy efficiency changes. The upgrades can be paid for via a finance deal on the electricity meter. From April 2018, if you want to rent your property privately, it will need to have an EPC rating of E or more. Ideally, make sure your property is as energy efficient as possible. To find out more and for a Q&A on the Green Deal, visit www.decc.gov.uk.

Rent	£7,400
Less Council Tax paid by landlord	£400
Net rent	£7,000
Wear and tear allowance (10 per cent)	£700

The alternative to 'wear and tear' is for you to claim the cost of replacing old items with a new equivalent (that is, not an improvement), minus any money you receive for selling the old one.

Furnished holiday lets in the UK and other EEA countries

Here you can claim a 'capital allowance' for the cost of each item of furniture and equipment you provide with the property, or you can claim a repairs allowance, as explained in Capital cost allowances, opposite. You can't claim wear and tear allowances.

Paperwork

Keep receipts and invoices for six years after the tax year they are for, so that you can substantiate any figures you put in your tax return. You'll need:

- Rent books.
- Receipts.
- Invoices.
- Bank statements (make sure you can separate your business and personal expenses).
- Details of dates when the property was let out.
- Details of other income for services provided to tenants.
- Details of your allowable expenses.
- Details of your capital costs.

How much can you claim?

Capital allowances vary depending on the item. From 6 April 2012, you can claim 100 per cent on the first £25,000 and 18 per cent on the rest.

Remember that you can only claim for items legitimately used in the business, or a fair proportion. For example, if you also live in half the property, you can only claim half the capital allowance.

Calculating profit

Your net profit is the figure remaining once you have deducted all allowable expenses from your rental income. Your taxable profit is this sum less any remaining personal allowances. This is added to your overall income and used to assess your total Income Tax. Income from more than one property is grouped together, but you have to work out holiday letting and overseas letting profits separately.

'Net profit is the figure remaining once all allowable expenses are deducted from the rental income. Taxable profit is this sum less any remaining personal allowances.'

For advice on working out your yield and return on investment see pages 43–5, which provide you with a detailed cost analysis and all the necessary calculations to work out these important figures.

Case study
Bill

Bill charges his lodger, Ben, £450 a month rent to share his house. As the annual rent of £5,400 is more than the Rent-a-Room allowance (£4,250), Bill has to decide how to deal with the income.

If he stays in the Rent-a-Room Scheme, over a year £4,250 of Ben's rent will be tax free. That leaves £1,150 to be taxed at Bill's top rate of tax, which is 20 per cent. So he pays tax of £230 on Ben's rent for the year.

He could, however, opt out of the Rent-a-Room Scheme and have the whole lot treated as ordinary rental income, which means he can deduct relevant expenses and have only the 'profit' taxed. The expenses Bill could claim against the rent come to about £2,500 for the year. When deducted from the total rent received, this would leave him with a profit of just £2,900 and a larger tax bill of £580 (20 per cent of £2,900).

Rent-a-Room Scheme

Rental income	£5,400
Rent-a-Room allowance	-£4,250
Profit	£1,150

Tax payable* = £1,150 x 20% = £230

Rental income

Rental income	£5,400
Expenses	-£2,500
Profit	£2,900

Tax payable* = £2,900 x 20% = £580

* If you are a 20% tax payer

What if you make a loss?

You can carry a loss forward to the next year and offset it against future profits as long as they are in the same property business. Losses on holiday lettings can also be offset against income in future years.

The Rent-a-Room Scheme

If you let a furnished room or rooms in your only or main home, you can choose to join the Rent-a-Room Scheme. This allows you to receive the first £4,250 a year free of tax, or £2,125 if you are letting jointly, but you cannot claim expenses on running the property or any capital allowances.

- **Your lodger can occupy a single room** or even a whole floor of your home, but it cannot be a separate flat.
- **You can join the Rent-a-Room Scheme** even if you are renting the property yourself: you do not have to own it, but you do need to operate within the terms of the lease (which may specify that you cannot have a lodger).
- **If you have a mortgage,** check whether renting out a room is within your lender's and insurer's terms and conditions.
- **You have to include any extra sums,** such as charges for meals, cleaning or laundry to give a

More details about the Rent-a-Room Scheme are available from **www.hmrc.gov.uk/manuals/pimmanual/pim4001.htm** and **www.gov.uk**.

total figure for receipts from your lodger.

- **If you don't normally receive a tax return** and your receipts are below the tax-free thresholds, you don't have to do anything. If your receipts go above the thresholds, you must tell your tax office.

You can choose year by year whether to use this scheme, according to whether it is to your advantage.

BE CAREFUL!

On the sale of a property, furnished holiday lets may be able to benefit from the new CGT entrepreneurs' relief, which could be up to £10 million in a person's lifetime, depending on how long you have owned the property/business. Seek specialist property tax advice so you can take advantage of any reliefs available.

Tax on holiday lets

Rules on tax for holiday lets are slightly different to those for residential lettings.

A holiday let must be:

- In the UK or other EEA country.
- Furnished.
- Available for letting for at least 210 days a year.
- Commercially let (not at cheap rates to family and friends) for at least 105 days a year, with each let not exceeding 31 days.

These rules for holiday lets apply for a seven-month period each year, meaning that you can let out the property on different terms, not as a holiday let, for the other five months if you wish. If you meet these criteria, you claim capital allowances rather than 'wear and tear'. This covers items such as:

- Furniture and furnishings.
- Equipment, such as refrigerators and washing machines.
- Machinery and plant used outside the property (such as vans and tools).

Any loss can be offset against your other income (reducing your overall tax bill) or carried forward.

Living abroad

If you move outside the UK for at least six months and let out your house, you must pay income tax on the rent, and can claim reliefs and allowances in much the same way as if you lived in the UK. You can choose which way to pay the tax:

- **Your letting agent or tenant** deducts tax from the rent at the basic rate each quarter and pays it direct to HMRC. You then set off the tax paid against your personal tax bill. Or:

If you live abroad, you can obtain further information from the Centre for non-residents at **www.hmrc.gov.uk/cnr**.

- **You apply to HMRC** to receive rent with no tax deducted and include it in your annual self-assessment form.

When, how and where to pay

If you are employed or receiving a PAYE pension and your taxable income from letting is under £2,500, your tax code can be adjusted to collect the tax payable. To do this, you will need to complete form P810 from your tax office. You don't need to tell HMRC about your rental income if you opt for the Rent-a-Room Scheme (see page 120) if this is below £2,500.

If your letting income is more than £2,500 and you are not on PAYE, you must fill in a self-assessment tax return. The quickest and easiest way to do this is online, because calculations are done for you and the filing deadlines are more generous than by post.

Case study Jack and Joanne

Jack is a bachelor and earns £90,000 in a well-paid city job, so is a 40 per cent tax payer. He met Joanne, the girl of his dreams, and soon they were married. Joanne gave up work shortly afterwards (she is therefore a 20 per cent tax payer) and they decided they could no longer live in Jack's one-bedroom city apartment, so they bought a new house and decided to rent out the existing apartment.

Jack transferred the apartment into joint ownership with Joanne, as 'tenants in common in unequal shares', with Joanne owning 90 per cent of the property. They filed a form 17 with their tax office, asking to be taxed on these proportions of the rental profit. Jack did this before they moved out of the flat to live in the new house.

The annual rental profit on the apartment was £4,000 per annum. This meant that Jack was taxed on £400 (10 per cent), and Joanne was taxed on £3,600 (90 per cent). Joanne had no tax liability as her £3,600 profit was covered by her personal tax allowance (£8,105 for 2012–13), whereas Jack had a £160 tax liability on his share of the profits. This meant that by transferring the property into unequal joint ownership, they would have an annual tax saving of £1,440 per annum. Over a ten-year period, this means a tax savings of £14,400!

NOTE: If there had been a mortgage on the flat, it is possible that there would be a liability to stamp duty land tax (SDLT) (see page 146) when Jack transferred a 90 per cent share in the property to Joanne. Joanne would be treated as taking over 90 per cent of the mortgage, and thus 'paying' Jack that amount for her share of the property. If this deemed payment was over the SDLT threshold (£125,000), then SDLT would be payable. Even if the amount of the mortgage was less than £125,000, the transfer would have to be notified to HMRC on Form SDLT 1.

Letting jointly

When letting jointly, both parties must show their share of income and expenses, and the profit or loss. HMRC provide an online guide called 'Property Income Manual'. If you are planning to live abroad for more than a few months while letting your home, you may need to read the HMRC's 'Non-resident Landlords Scheme'.

Income tax savings can occur by letting property jointly. This is particularly the case if you pay tax at 40 per cent and your spouse (or civil partner) pays no tax, or tax at 20 per cent. In this scenario, it really does make sense to own the property jointly. This is because you will be passing on a portion of the rental profit to your spouse, who will be able to use his/her annual income tax personal allowance (see the case study opposite).

A married couple (or civil partnership) are deemed to receive equal shares of income from jointly owned property, unless they in fact own it in a different proportion, and elect (using form 17) to be taxed in that proportion.

Capital Gains Tax (CGT) planning

A property investor is likely to incur a Capital Gains Tax (CGT) liability in the following two situations:

- **When a property is sold at a higher price** than that for which it was purchased.
- **When a property, or part of a property, is transferred** to anyone other than a spouse or civil partner – in such a case the person making the gift will be treated as if he had sold the property (or part of the property) for its market value on the date of the transfer.

The tax is paid on the gain made and can be as high as 28 per cent of that gain. This means that on a £100,000 gain, the CGT payable could be up to £28,000.

This does depend on whether you are a higher or lower rate tax payer and there are two reliefs that can reduce the amount of tax you owe.

Tenants in common

Many people don't realise that, in most cases, when buying with a partner or spouse, your property should be bought as tenants in common, not joint tenants. This is especially significant if you are business partners and if you are married and want to pass your properties onto your children. Seek professional wealth and tax advice to best mitigate your property tax bill.

For more information on property tax go to: **www.gov.uk** (search for 'Tax on property'), **www.hmrc.gov.uk**, **www.property-tax-portal.co.uk** and **www.nicholsonsca.co.uk**.

Strategies for reducing Capital Gains Tax

- Use the '36 Month Rule': Provided that a house has at some time been your main residence, the last three years of ownership are deemed to be a period when it was your main residence, regardless of where you actually lived during that period. If you purchased a property in January 2003 and lived in it as your main residence until the end of December 2005, when you moved out and let the property, then provided you sold the property before the end of December 2008, there will be no CGT liability.
- Use joint ownership: If a property is jointly owned, then each person will be able to use the annual CGT allowance, which is £10,600 for the 2012-13 tax year.
- Benefit from living in and letting a property: If you have lived in and also let a property, then you can benefit from letting relief, which can be as much as £40,000.

'There are two reliefs that can be used to reduce the amount of CGT: only or main residence relief and letting relief.'

Personal CGT allowance

Every individual has an annual CGT allowance. For the tax year 2012-13 this is £10,600. This can be deducted from the total gains you make in the tax year. Over this amount, the tax is a flat rate of 18 or 28 per cent.

Only or Main Residence (OMR) relief

This tax relief is available if the property was used as your main residence. This relief is calculated based on how long the property was your OMR. The longer the property was your OMR, the greater the relief will be. Ultimately, if the property was your OMR for the whole period of ownership, then all the gain made on the property will be exempt from tax.

If a property has ever been your OMR, then it is deemed to be so for the last three years of your ownership of it. This is the case whether or not you actually live there during that period.

Letting relief

This potential relief is available if the property satisfies the following two conditions:

- **The property was your OMR** at some time during your ownership of it.
- **The property has been let out** as residential accommodation when it was not your OMR.

The calculation of this relief is quite complicated, but essentially up to £40,000 (or, in the case of a jointly owned house, £40,000 for each owner) of gains can be treated as exempt from tax. To check if this relief applies to you, see document HS283 'Private residence relief' on www.hmrc.gov.uk/helpsheets/hs283.pdf.

Comparing a company versus an individual let

	Company	Individual
Rental profit	50,000	50,000
Company admin	(1,000)	NIL
Taxable profit	49,000	50,000
Tax at 20%*/40%	(9,800)	(20,000)
Cash after tax	39,200	30,000
Tax on dividend	(9,800)	N/A
Cash in hand	29,400	30,000

Forming a property company

If you intend to build up a significant portfolio of let properties by ploughing the rental profits back into buying other properties, then you may wish to consider setting up a limited company to hold the properties. The information given here can only be a brief outline of what this entails. If you are thinking of making this change, consult your accountant and property tax specialist for more information.

Using a limited company

Deciding to add buy to let to your current income and tax circumstances or to create a company is a major and complicated decision. Part of that decision depends on how and why you are investing in property and, as each set of circumstances is individual, it is essential that from the start you consult a property tax expert or two to ensure you are making the right decision.

Limited companies pay corporation tax (CT) on their profits (both income and capital gains). The rate of CT depends on the level of profits for the year, but for profits up to £300,000, the rate is 20 per cent in 2012–13. If you are a 40 per cent taxpayer, then by owning your property through a company, the tax payable on the rental profits will be 20 per cent lower. This is not the whole story, however.

After the company has paid CT on its profits, the remaining cash is still in the company. Generally, the most tax-efficient way to extract this cash is by the company paying dividends to its shareholders. The additional income tax on a dividend for a 40 per cent taxpayer is 25 per cent of the dividend. However, in any company, the circumstances of the directors and shareholders need to be considered fully in determining the most tax-efficient strategy.

You must also remember that a company is a more formal structure, and that there will be costs associated with running it – these are likely to be around £1,000 per year for even the simplest company.

If you are going to draw all the cash out of the company by way of dividends, it is likely that you will make little or no savings (see the table, page 125).

If, however, you intend to reinvest the profits rather than extract them from the company, you will see from the same table that after paying its CT, the company has £9,200 more available to reinvest than the individual does. This means that a company can provide a good vehicle for growing your portfolio of properties, because you have more cash left to reinvest. But if you intend to draw out your profits for other expenditure, there is little or no saving to be made by using a company.

‘A company has a more formal structure and there are costs associated with running it, which will amount to around £1,000 per year for even the simplest one.’

Tenancy law

Before looking at specific types of tenancy in greater detail, it is important to understand the definitions of key legal words and phrases and know something about the history of tenancy Acts in both the private and public sectors. When considering the legal aspects of tenancy law, it is important to seek independent, legal advice from a tenancy law expert.

Private-sector tenancies

The law is different for private-sector tenancies according to when the tenancy began – see the chart below, which sets out the differences.

Rent Act tenancies

Residential tenancies that began before 15 January 1989 are governed by the Rent Act 1977, which gave most tenants very good security of tenure. Thousands of Rent Act tenancies originally entered into prior to 15 January 1989 are still running.

Their terms stay in force even if, as a tenant, you were granted a new tenancy by your landlord after this date and if you have since moved to another property owned by the same landlord. This rule also applies if a new landlord buys the property, provided there is no gap between the end of the original Rent Act tenancy and the granting of a new one.

If you are buying a property, particularly at auction, you must make sure you fully investigate the type of tenancy as it may well

Tenant Acts since 1977

Act	Implementation	Type of tenancy	Other information
Rent Act 1977	Until 15 January 1989	Protected or statutory tenancies	Tenant has full security of tenure and can control the amount of rent paid
Housing Act 1988	15 January 1989 to 28 February 1997	Either ordinary assured tenancy or assured shorthold tenancy (also known as 'old' shortholds) with a minimum fixed term of six months	Tenant has full security of tenure with the ordinary assured tenancy, but no security after fixed term has elapsed on the assured shorthold tenancy; there is some protection for the tenant against excessive rent
Housing Act 1996	On or after 28 February 1997	Assured shorthold tenancy	There is no security of tenure after the fixed term has expired

Some legal definitions

Fixed or ascertainable period

The period of a tenancy or lease must be defined from the outset, stipulating when it is to begin and when or how it is to end. Although the tenancy of a periodic letting can go on indefinitely, either party can terminate it by giving notice to quit, which expires at the end of a relevant week or month, meeting the requirement of certainty that the arrangement will end at some point.

Grounds for possession

Grounds for possession may be cited in possession proceedings against a tenant when a landlord wants to regain possession of his or her property. There are separate grounds for possession relating to assured tenancies and public-sector tenancies. They were laid down in the Housing Act 1988, as amended by the Housing Act 1996. Landlords may also seek possession when it can be demonstrated that a tenant is no longer using the accommodation as his or her principal home.

Lease

The same as a tenancy, but the term is usually used to indicate that the property is let for a fixed term, such as six months or a certain number of years, while the word 'tenancy' suggests periodic letting from week to week or month to month.

Licence

If the occupier is only given the right to share the property (for example, with the owner) rather than have exclusive use of a specific part of it, the arrangement would be a licence, not a lease or a tenancy. This is an important point because tenants have far greater statutory legal protection than licensees.

Security of tenure

Gives the tenant an indefinite right to stay, unless the landlord has specific grounds for eviction.

Tenancy

An arrangement with two key requirements: the letting is for a 'fixed or ascertainable period of time' and it grants 'exclusive possession' of the property. Although this is usually in return for rent, such a charge is not legally part of the tenancy.

have this type of arrangement in place. Among the terms to watch out for are:

- **The landlord cannot take possession** of the property without providing a 'ground' or 'grounds' for doing so.
- **If the tenant dies,** their tenancy could be passed on to their relatives if they lived in the property for a certain period before the death. There are a number of restrictions in place and the tenancy usually becomes an assured, rather than statutory one.
- **The amount of rent is controlled by rent officers,** who generally set a 'fair rent' below the market level, which cannot then be changed for two years.

Protection is given to 'protected tenancies', which subsequently become 'statutory tenancies'.

A protected tenancy exists where a house was 'let as a separate dwelling', which does not have to be the tenant's only home, while the tenant does not have to be an individual: it could be a limited company. Protected tenants have rent control and succession rights, but they don't necessarily have security of tenure (see page 129), which would require them to be a statutory tenant.

At the end of a protected tenancy, the tenant will become a statutory tenant with security of tenure only 'if and so long as he occupies the dwelling house as his residence'. Now he can only be evicted once the landlord has been to court and established one of the grounds for possession (see pages 160–2). Statutory tenants must be individuals.

Certain tenancies are excluded from this legislation. For example, if the landlord is a resident landlord living in another part of the same building containing the rented

Tenant's take

While it was deeply unpopular with landlords, the Rent Act offered admirable protection for tenants. If you are still covered by it, you have security of tenure and your rent is likely to be set below the market rate. These terms are likely to be handed on to your spouse when you die, and other relatives can still benefit from them, although they are likely to be entitled only to an assured, rather than protected tenancy. However, you should always seek professional advice if you have any queries or need to confirm your situation for any reason. As for landlords, this is a complex legal area and if you feel your rights are being affected, consult Citizens Advice, Shelter or a solicitor.

If you have any legal queries, use your legal representative, Shelter (**www.shelter.org**) or Citizens Advice. To find your nearest Citizens Advice branch, go to **www.adviceguide.org.uk** or your local phone book.

accommodation, subject to certain conditions, the tenant will have none of the rights granted to Rent Act or Housing Act tenants. See pages 138–9 for more information.

The Rent Act protected tenants but made it almost impossible for landlords to operate profitably, many of whom stopped letting altogether. As a result, new legislation was passed in 1988 that radically changed the law regarding tenancy to encourage more private landlords.

Housing Act 1988 tenancies

The Housing Act 1988 came into force on 15 January 1989 and remained so until 28 February 1997. This legislation covers assured tenancies and assured shorthold tenancies and gives landlords a choice on how much security of tenure they give. There are still many tenancies in existence that began during this period.

Ordinary assured tenancy

An ordinary assured tenancy (so-called to distinguish it from an assured shorthold tenancy), gives tenants some security of tenure because the landlord has to cite a ground for possession before taking back the property, even if the term agreed between both parties has expired. It does not restrict how much rent can be charged. Any new letting to an existing ordinary assured tenant will remain an ordinary assured tenancy whenever it was granted, even if it was after 28 February 1997 when the legislation was changed.

However, the tenant can serve a notice on the landlord that he wants the new tenancy to be a shorthold. This rule was introduced to allow a compromise when a landlord had a ground for possession (see page 168), and would discontinue the action in return for giving the tenant a new, shorthold letting (see overleaf), thus ensuring the tenant still had accommodation, albeit with less secure tenancy.

Although this is possible, it is questionable that it would be in the tenant's best interests to do so as it is sometimes difficult to obtain a final possession order relying on a discretionary possession ground, and therefore the tenant may be best taking their chances at a possession hearing.

> **'It pays to understand the difference between types of tenancy regardless of whether you are a landlord or tenant.'**

Periodic tenancy

A periodic tenancy comes into being when a landlord doesn't reclaim possession at the end of an original assured shorthold tenancy nor does he issue a new tenancy agreement. The terms and conditions of the original assured shorthold tenancy agreement remain in place, as does the landlord's right to bring the tenancy to an end by service of the required two months from the date the rent started.

Assured shorthold tenancy

An assured shorthold tenancy has to be for at least six months (but could have a fixed term of many years despite its name), after which the landlord is entitled to claim possession through a court order, should the need arise. If the tenancy is granted after 28 February 1997, a landlord cannot obtain an order for possession which takes effect until at least six months after the tenancy started. There is some protection for tenants against excessive rent.

To regain possession, the landlord was required to serve the tenant with a prescribed form of notice informing them of the consequences of the tenancy being shorthold at the commencement of the tenancy. If they didn't do this, the tenancy was regarded as an ordinary (or fully) assured tenancy, which offers full security of tenure. Many landlords who did not comply properly with this rule found they were unable to evict tenants even when the six-month term expired.

If the parties are the same, a new tenancy of the same (or almost the same) property will be deemed to be shorthold unless the landlord informs the tenant in writing that it is not. In such cases, as no shorthold notices have to be served, the letting need not be for a fixed term, and if it is, the term can be less than six months.

Housing Act 1996 tenancies

The Housing Act was amended in 1996. After 28 February 1997, most private tenancies have been assured shorthold unless the landlord opts for an ordinary assured tenancy (see page 131).

'If a tenancy was granted after 28 February 1997, a landlord cannot obtain an order for possession until at least six months after its start.'

BE CAREFUL!

If a landlord lets a property on an assured tenancy, the tenant has the right to remain in the property unless the landlord can prove there are grounds for possession. The landlord does not have the right to just repossess the property when the tenancy comes to an end.

Public-sector tenancies

The Housing Act 1988 brought registered social landlord tenancies into the private sector on or after 15 January 1989, and these tenants have either (mostly) an assured tenancy or (sometimes) an assured shorthold tenancy.

Assured tenants have security of tenure as the landlord must provide a statutory ground for possession under the 1988 Act if he or she wishes to evict a tenant. There is no legal control over rent increases, even though one of the aims of housing associations is to let at affordable rents. Registered providers of social housing should provide their tenants with a written agreement specifying the level of rents to be charged and the conditions of the tenancy. The Tenant Services Authority (TSA) has produced a set of standards that specify the delivery requirements by social housing landlords. Broadly speaking these are created in conjunction with the priorities of the local tenant communities they serve.

Other public-sector landlords include housing action trusts, which aim to improve and modernise council housing prior to transferring or selling it. Many local authorities have transferred some or all of their housing stock to registered providers of social housing.

Housing associations are non-profit-making bodies that provide affordable accommodation and these organisations are one of the major providers of state-funded housing.

- **Some associations are registered with the Homes and Communities Agency** or with the Welsh Assembly.

'Assured tenants have security of tenure as the tenancy relates to the 1988 Act.'

For more information, visit **www.homesandcommunities.co.uk** and for the Welsh Assembly go to **www.wales.gov.uk**. The grounds for possession for an assured tenancy are on pages 168–9 and those for possession for a public-sector tenancy are on pages 170–1.

- **Some associations (but not all) are registered charities** and have their own charitable rules as well.
- **Others are run on a co-operative basis** where tenants themselves own and manage the properties.

The law relating to security of tenure and rent control will depend on the type of housing association and the date when tenancy was granted. Those begun before 15 January 1989 are dealt with differently to those commencing on or after that date. If you want to compare how your current registered provider of social housing performs, visit www.homesandcommunities.co.uk to find out how tenants rate their social housing service.

Some housing associations choose not to register and retain their independence so that they can set up shared-ownership schemes. This means they do not qualify for state funding and are not supervised by a government body. After 15 January 1989, they are governed by the same rules as registered providers of social housing (see above), except they do not have the benefits of a 'tenant's guarantee'. These come under the protection of the Rent Act 1977.

'Some housing associations aren't registered, which means they aren't supervised by a government body.'

The chapter on social lets (see pages 149–56) answers the most frequently asked questions by landlords and tenants on the subject of social (or public-sector) lets.

Assured shorthold tenancies

8

Nearly every letting begun on or after 28 February 1997 will be an assured shorthold tenancy, which gives no security of tenure when the contractual letting term ends. The landlord can also obtain possession without having to give a reason, provided he follows the correct procedure (see pages 160–71).

The landlord's viewpoint

Assured shorthold tenancies suit landlords because they have the absolute right to possession (see pages 164–5). This means that possession can be obtained faster and cheaper than under normal court procedures.

BE CAREFUL!

Are you a prospective tenant rather than landlord? Read this section, too, as there is useful advice here for both sides of the tenancy agreement.

Assured shorthold tenancies mean that a landlord can get his property back during the tenancy under certain circumstances, such as if the rent is not being paid, as long as a special term has been incorporated into the letting agreement.

How does a tenancy qualify as a shorthold?

Various conditions have to be fulfilled for a tenancy to qualify as a shorthold in a house let as a separate dwelling:

- The tenant or each of the joint tenants is an individual.
- The tenant, or at least one of the joint tenants, occupies the house as his only or principal home.
- The tenancy is not specifically excluded by other provisions of the Housing Act 1988.

Jargon buster

Tenancy The letting must be a tenancy, not simply a licence to occupy the property

House This is any building designed or adapted for living in, so the term includes flats, barns, etc.

Let as a separate dwelling The property cannot be let for business purposes, and must be 'a' single dwelling (not, for example, a house converted into several flats – although each of these separate flats could fall within the definition). It must be 'separate', which boils down to whether the tenant regards and treats it as 'home'. For example, a single room could qualify as a dwelling even if the tenant has the right to share other rooms, such as a kitchen or a bathroom. If the facilities are shared with the landlord, the tenancy would not be seen as an assured or shorthold tenancy because it has a 'resident landlord' (see pages 138–9).

The key point is that the tenant must have the right to exclusive possession of one part of the house. If the property is simply shared by the occupiers who are left to decide between themselves who has which bedroom, they are licensees rather than tenants.

Can any property be used for an assured shorthold tenancy?

There are a number of exceptions that are excluded from the definition of an assured tenancy:

- **Tenancies entered into before 15 January 1989.**
- **High value properties:** for tenancies granted before 1 April 1990, the cut-off point is a rateable value of more than £750 (£1,500 in Greater London). After that date, the tenancy is excluded if the rent payable is £100,000 or more per annum.
- **Low rent:** on lettings made before 1 April 1990, if the annual rent is less than two-thirds of the rateable value. Since that date, the exclusion applies if the rent does not exceed £250 per annum (£1,000 in Greater London).
- **Business tenancies:** if the premises are occupied for the purpose of business. So a traditional corner shop with living accommodation for staff over it would be excluded.
- **Tenancies of agricultural land,** although such tenants will probably have other statutory rights under legislation on agricultural holdings.
- **Lettings to students:** lettings to students by educational bodies, such as universities and colleges. This exception does not apply to lettings by landlords other than the institutions themselves.
- **Holiday lettings:** a holiday let cannot be an assured tenancy.
- **Lettings by resident landlords,** when the landlord lives in another part of the building occupied by the tenant.
- **Crown, local authority and housing association lettings:** although they may have other protections (see the next chapter on pages 149–56).

'For an assured shorthold tenancy to conform, the tenant must have exclusive possession of one part of the house.'

If you are a tenant, and your needs aren't met on these pages, turn to pages 145–8, where frequently asked questions by tenants are answered. For social lets, see pages 149–56.

Do I need to get planning permission to alter a property?

If you are converting a house into several flats, planning permission will be required for change of use from occupation by one family to occupation by tenants, and it will probably be needed for the building works, too. If you are not converting a house, but are letting it to a group of people (such as students), rather than as a family home, this could also represent a material change of use. Ask for advice from your local planning office. See also the advice on HMOs on page 31.

Which would be better – an assured shorthold tenancy or an ordinary assured tenancy?

Most landlords let on a shorthold basis because they can regain possession of the property more easily when they want to, and because, if they are borrowing money to purchase the property, the lender will insist on it. However, if you are letting the house in which you have lived at some time in the past (not necessarily recently), you may want to consider an ordinary assured tenancy. These normally give the tenant full security of tenure, but if you previously lived in the property, there is a mandatory ground for possession so you could still get your property back.

Offering permanent security to a tenant through an assured tenancy can tie up your assets in a property you cannot gain possession of, and so there is a danger that you cannot realise your investment.

I've heard mention of the 'resident landlord exception'. What is this?

The majority of lettings by resident landlords occupying another part of the same building are not assured or shorthold tenancies and their tenants have no security and few rights under the legislation protecting them from eviction. This is known as the 'resident landlord exception'.

The main significance for this is with regard to lettings entered into before 28 February 1997, after which all tenancies are shortholds with no security of tenure anyway. In the case of these later lettings, the effect of the resident landlord rule will be that:

- The tenant cannot refer the rent to the rent assessment committee (RAC) (see below).
- The tenant is not entitled to two months' notice terminating the shorthold.
- The tenant may not benefit from protection-from-eviction legislation.

The RAC is a local panel with the power to set a maximum rent on a property on behalf of the council. Visit **www.gov.uk** for more information and see also page 145.

- Statutory succession provisions do not apply.
- Statutory rules on increasing the rent and not assigning will not apply.

For the letting to be excluded from the definition of an assured or shorthold tenancy all of these conditions must apply:

- The house that is let must form only part of the building.
- The building must not be a purpose-built block of flats.
- The tenancy must have been granted by an individual (that is, not a limited company) who at the time of the grant occupied another part of the same building as his only or principal home.
- At all times since the tenancy was granted, the interest of the landlord has continued to belong to an individual who continued so to reside.

So the resident landlord exception applies when the tenant lives in a part of the same building as you, the landlord, provided it is not a purpose-built block of flats. A landlord living in a large house that is partly let out, or converted into several flats, is outside the definition.

You must be in occupation throughout the tenancy and if you move out, the exception no longer applies. If you are letting jointly, only one needs to be in residence at any time. Absences for holidays or illness, or at times of change or death of the landlord or change of ownership, are permitted. If the tenant has an assured tenancy during which the landlord moves in and subsequently grants a further tenancy, the exception does not apply.

'Offering permanent security to a tenant by an assured tenancy can tie up your assets for years.'

How should I confirm a tenancy?

It makes enormous sense to arrange the tenancy using a written tenancy agreement – there are examples of clauses at the back of this book. This will help avoid disputes over the terms of the let. Perhaps surprisingly, such a deed is not legally essential in most cases (a tenancy can be granted orally in many typical circumstances) and many residential lettings are entered into quite informally, but it is highly advisable to put the arrangement in writing in the form of a deed.

The agreement must be signed and the signatures witnessed, and it should end 'signed as a deed'. It is best if two identical copies of the tenancy agreement are drawn up and signed, one for the tenant, the other for you. Your copy is the actual lease, and the tenant's copy is called the counterpart.

Should the agreement be for a fixed term?

Most shorthold tenancies are for a fixed term of either six or 12 months. If it is longer, the tenant can get the rent checked by the legally binding decision of the rent assessment committee and you could be stuck with a tenant paying a rent which inflation has seriously eroded in value.

If you wish to let for a shorter period, such as three months, remember that under a shorthold, the courts cannot order possession before six months have passed since the tenancy began.

You may intend to sell or occupy the house yourself by a particular date, but bear in mind that although a shorthold tenancy has no security of tenure, not all tenants leave voluntarily at the end of a let. If this were the case, you would have to obtain a court order for possession. Although this is a formality, it will take three or more months and you may want to allow for this when you decide the length of the tenancy.

If you don't have a fixed date for when you want the property back, you can let it on a periodic tenancy, which can be either weekly or monthly. This allows you to continue the letting for several years. If you choose to, you can also change the rental charge whenever you like.

With a fixed-term tenancy, you will only be able to charge the agreed rent at the end of the term.

What terms should be included in a shorthold tenancy agreement?

The agreement should include:

- **A description of the property,** clearly indicating the number or precise location of a flat, for example.
- **Details of how the rent is to be paid:** The common law implication is that rent is payable in arrears, unless the contract expressly says it should be paid in advance. If weekly intervals are chosen, you must provide a rent book. Intervals should be weekly, fortnightly, monthly, quarterly or yearly.
- **Interest on arrears:** If the rent falls into arrears, you cannot claim interest on it until you start court proceedings. This problem can be overcome by including a term that allows you to add interest to any arrears at a specified, reasonable rate.
- **Council Tax:** The tenant is liable for Council Tax unless the property is an HMO (see page 31), in which case you must pay, adding a figure to cover it to the rental charge. In such a case, the agreement should include provision to increase the rent to take into account any rise in Council Tax. Otherwise, the agreement should stipulate that the rent is exclusive of Council Tax and requiring the tenant to pay it or reimburse you should you become responsible for its payment.

- **Water charges:** In the absence of a clause to the contrary, it is assumed that the tenant pays these, although the landlord often pays on short-term lettings. If so, there should be some provision allowing for a rent increase should the water charges go up.
- **Repairs and decoration:** The Landlord and Tenant Act 1985 imposes an obligation on you to repair, for example, the structure and exterior of the property where the tenancy is for a term less than seven years. However, a provision should be included allocating responsibility for non-structural internal repairs and decoration. Without this, neither party would have any obligation to do this. It is reasonable to impose the liability for these matters on the tenant if the term is for more than 12 months, but not if the let is shorter than that, unless the repairs are necessary because of the tenant's acts or neglect. If the property has a garden, it is worth including an obligation on the tenant to maintain it or at least cut any grass.
- **Alterations:** It is essential to prohibit the tenant from making alterations to the house, even if he considers them to be improvements, unless approved by you.
- **Use:** It is standard to restrict the use of the property to that of a single private dwelling and impose obligations not to cause nuisance or annoyance to the neighbours or to damage the house or its contents.
- **Assignment and subletting:** See page 143 for guidance on these points.
- **Address for service:** Section 48 of the Landlord and Tenant Act 1987 states that no rent is lawfully due from a tenant unless and until you give the tenant in writing an address in England or Wales at which notices can be served upon him. It makes sense to include this address in the agreement. It can be your solicitor's or the letting agent's.
- **Deposit:** Within 14 days of when the tenant paid the deposit, your agent or you should supply:
  - Your or your agent's contact details.
  - Which tenancy deposit scheme is being used (see pages 83–6) and the contact details for the scheme.
  - Information about the purpose of a tenancy deposit.

Use the explanation of these terms in conjunction with the examples of clauses given on pages 190–204.

  - Information about how the tenant needs to apply to get the deposit back at the end of the tenancy.
  - What the tenant can do should there be a dispute about the deposit.

All this information can either be within the agreement or provided in a separate document or letter.

- **Rent increases:** See page 82.
- **Break clauses:** This is a term allowing the party specified to bring the lease to an end before it has run its full length and may be appropriate in a fixed-term tenancy. The break clause allows you to terminate the tenancy if you, or a member of your family:
  - Wish to occupy the house or you want to sell with vacant possession.
  - If you die and your personal representatives need to obtain possession.

If this clause is included, there should be a tenant's break clause too, or the agreement is likely to fall foul of the Unfair Terms Regulations (see page 158).

- **Children and pets:** If you want to prohibit these, it must be expressly stated in the agreement and ideally when you advertise the property at the start. However, you will want to avoid breaking the Unfair Terms Regulations (see also page 158). Unattended pets left to roam the property during the day can cause damage, so dogs and cats are often not allowed without consent – which can also be offered for pets kept in secure cages. It would be unlawful to prevent a blind or deaf person from keeping their guide or hearing dog in the house.
- **Forfeiture:** A forfeiture clause is essential in any fixed-term

Get it in writing

'Get it in writing' is the golden rule with many dealings, none more so than letting, yet many tenancies are still granted orally, and this often leads to disputes when the two parties differ about what was agreed. The Housing Act 1996 places an obligation on the landlord of a new shorthold tenancy to provide the tenant with a statement of at least the more important terms of the tenancy, which include:

- The tenancy commencement date.
- The rent payable and the due dates.
- Any terms providing for rent review.
- The length of a fixed-term tenancy.

If these are not provided, the tenant should request them in writing. It is then a criminal offence for you to fail to give the information within 28 days without a reasonable excuse. The Act makes it clear that the statement by you is not to be regarded as conclusive evidence of what was agreed, and your version can be challenged by the tenant.

'The golden rule with many dealings, especially tenancies, is to get it down in writing.'

assured tenancy of any length, including a shorthold (it would not apply to an assured tenancy). The clause permits you to end a fixed-term lease before it ends if the tenant fails to comply with agreed obligations, such as paying the rent. Some of the assured tenancy grounds for possession can be used to end a fixed-term tenancy provided the tenancy agreement makes clear provision for this, stating which grounds are considered to apply. As always, it is important that these clauses are written in clear plain English: many traditionally worded forfeiture clauses could be declared void because they are incomprehensible to all but lawyers.

Can a tenant transfer or sublet the tenancy?

The 1988 Act suggests that the tenant shall not assign or sublet any part of the property without your consent. This statutory prohibition does not apply if a premium was paid on the grant or renewal of the tenancy. A premium is any money payments in addition to rent or a returnable deposit worth more than one-sixth of the annual rent. Statutory prohibition does not prevent taking in lodgers or sharing with another person. You have no obligation to be reasonable in deciding if you will give consent.

Because these statutory restrictions do not apply to fixed-term tenancies, there is a potential problem for landlords granting assured shortholds. While the assured shorthold tenant has no security of tenure, the person he sublets to could arguably have an assured tenancy with full security of tenure and this security could be binding on the landlord. To avoid the problem, make sure the tenancy agreement contains an express provision prohibiting subletting, while allowing assignment of the lease with the landlord's consent.

Periodic tenancies

There are specific provisions in the Housing Act 1988 regarding succession of periodic tenancies on the death of a sole tenant and these override other inheritance laws. The tenancy passes to the tenant's spouse provided they have been occupying the property as their principal home immediately prior to the death. The couple do not have to have been married and can be of the same sex.

These succession rights do not apply if the deceased tenant was a successor themselves - through this rule, by inheritance, as the sole survivor of joint tenants, or under the provisions of the Rent Act 1977. Therefore, only one statutory succession is possible. If there is no qualifying 'spouse' or if the tenancy has already succeeded one, the tenancy passes on under the will or intestacy of the deceased as already explained.

What happens if the tenant dies?

In the case of a fixed-term tenancy, since the tenant owns the tenancy, it can be passed on in the same way as the deceased's other property. If he or she is a joint tenant, the other becomes the sole tenant, but on the death of a sole tenant, the right to live in the property goes to the person nominated in the will. If the tenant dies without a will, ownership is decided by the laws of inheritance.

What happens if a tenant's children become adults?

It is worth seeking advice from a legal lettings expert at this stage as it is likely you will need to add them to the tenancy agreement.

How do I obtain possession?

The court must order possession on or after the ending of a shorthold, provided you follow the correct procedure, serving a Section 21 notice and giving at least two months' notice that you require possession of your property.

What are the grounds for possession?

As a shorthold is a type of assured tenancy, the mandatory and discretionary grounds that apply to ordinary assured tenancies also apply. But as you have right to possession under a shorthold, you would not normally need to use these grounds.

However, the normal shorthold procedure to obtain possession can be used only after the expiry of any fixed-term granted. So if a 12-month fixed term was granted, possession under the shorthold procedure can only be obtained at its end. This could pose a serious problem if a tenant is not paying the rent.

A solution here is offered by the fact that some of the ordinary assured tenancy grounds can be used during a fixed term, including mandatory ground 8 and discretionary grounds 10 and 11 (see pages 168–9). All of these deal with rent arrears. As with other assured tenancies, these grounds can be used during the fixed term only if the tenancy agreement contains provision for their use. Without such provision, you cannot obtain possession from a defaulting tenant until the end of the fixed term: you could sue the tenant for arrears, but with no guarantee of payment.

Faced with a periodic shorthold tenant who won't pay the rent, you can use the normal shorthold procedure for obtaining possession and immediately serve the usual two months' notice (see pages 160–1). As stated, possession can still not be ordered until the tenancy has run for six months.

Chapter 10, Legal action, beginning on page 157, explains the procedure for taking possession of a property. The grounds for possession are also listed in this chapter, on pages 168–9.

The tenant's take

If you are a landlord, you will find there is information in this section that is every bit as useful for you as for the tenant. Rent levels, stamp duty land tax and ending an agreement are the main subjects that are discussed here.

How much rent can I be charged?

Under a shorthold tenancy, there is no restriction on how much rent can be charged, so market forces will prevail. You may have the right to challenge the amount originally agreed by referring it to the Rent Assessment Committee (RAC) – a local panel with the power to set a maximum rent on a property on behalf of the council. You can do this at any time during your first shorthold term. The landlord can only raise the rent if he follows the right procedure. He cannot do this without your consent, unless the terms of the tenancy include a provision for rent increase.

In a fixed-term tenancy, there are also no statutory provisions for setting a rent increase, so a landlords might well include provision for it if your tenancy lasts longer than, say, 12 months. Even then, you can still refer the original rent to the RAC.

At the end of the fixed term, you continue in possession as a statutory periodic tenant and the landlord can follow the procedure outlined above. Alternatively, at the end of the shorthold the landlord can take up his or her absolute right to possession and grant a new tenancy at a higher rent. You would then have an unenviable choice of agreeing a higher rent or losing your home. See www.gov.uk for more information.

Call out the RAC

If you feel you have signed up to pay an over-the-odds rent, you can go to arbitration from the local Rent Assessment Committee (RAC). Depending on your tenancy, there are deadlines you need to apply by. For regulated tenancies refer to the VOA. The committee then compares rents being charged for similar properties and sets the tariff at what it considers the market rate. A lower rent is fixed only if it is felt the landlord is charging 'significantly' more than he should.

If it is a fixed-term tenancy, the rent becomes the maximum chargeable for the remainder of the term, however long it is - a good reason for landlords not to agree to five-year shortholds.

In the case of a periodic tenancy, the rent is fixed and the landlord must wait 12 months after the assessment before he can increase it using the statutory procedure (see page 89). However, as he has an absolute right to possession, he could give two months' notice and start a new tenancy at whatever rate he desires.

In the case of periodic (that is, weekly or monthly) tenancies, there is, however, provision for the landlord to raise the rent even when not permitted to do so by the tenancy agreement. It is a complex procedure requiring the landlord to serve a notice on you in a prescribed form stating a new rental figure. If you don't agree the figure, you can take it to arbitration with the local RAC.

'Under a shorthold tenancy, there is no restriction on how much rent can be charged.'

Do I have to pay stamp duty land tax (SDLT)?

Stamp Duty has changed its name to Stamp Duty Land Tax (SDLT). In the past it was a voluntary tax for the landlord, but is now a compulsory tax to be paid by you, the tenant.

SDLT becomes liable when you take a lease that exceeds £125,000. As a result, unless you take a particularly long lease, or are renting at extremely high costs, it is unlikely that you will have to pay it.

Below are two examples of how the tax might be levied. However, the rules are complicated, so seek independent advice from an experienced letting agent, Her Majesty's Revenue & Customs (HMRC) or a property tax specialist. Even if it appears you are likely to need to pay SDLT, it may be possible to reduce the amount owed.

Example 1

Mr Pragel rents a property for 12 months at a monthly rent of £1,000. The rental value over the period of the lease is £12,000. The rental value is less than £125,000, so no SDLT is payable by the tenant.

Example 2

Mr Locum rents a property for £4,000 per month for a three-year period. The amount of the lease is therefore 12 months x £4,000 = £48,000 per year. Over the three-year period of the lease, this would mean the value of the lease is £48,000 x 3 years = £144,000. This would exceed the SDLT threshold and trigger a payment, which would be calculated as follows: £144,000 – £125,000 = £19,000.

SDLT is charged at 1 per cent of the amount of the lease in excess of £125,000, so would be calculated: £19,000 x 1% = £190.

For more information on SDLT, visit **www.hmrc.gov.uk/so/sdlt/index.htm** or you can call 0845 603 0135 for advice.

Is there any regulation for the way a contract is written?

The Unfair Terms in Consumer Contracts Regulations cover all consumer contracts, including tenancy agreements, but not company lets, and declare that any terms that have not been individually negotiated and which can be considered unfair to the tenant would be void. A term is unfair if it tips the contract against the consumer (you, the tenant) in favour of the business (the landlord).

Examples of clauses that would be open to challenge include:

- A requirement to pay an excessive deposit.
- Penalty clauses for the late payment of rent.
- Clauses giving the landlord the right to enter the premises without reasonable notice.
- Provisions allowing for arbitrary increases in rent.
- Clauses making you pay unreasonable costs.
- Total prohibitions on assigning and subletting.

In addition, the agreement should be in clear language without the use of legal jargon or words with special meanings that you don't know. See also 'What terms should be included in a shorthold tenancy agreement?' on pages 140–2.

Can I transfer or sublet the tenancy?

In theory, a tenancy belongs to its signatory like any other possession and can be 'assigned' (sold or given away) to anyone you choose, or you can grant a lease shorter than your own (sublet) or take in lodgers. Not surprisingly, a landlord who has carefully vetted you will not be best pleased to find his property sublet to someone he has never even met, so most tenancy agreements expressly forbid assignment and/or subletting.

Trying to prohibit both risks contravening the Unfair Terms in Consumer Contracts Regulations, so landlords tend to allow assigning or subletting on the condition that it is with their consent. This allows the landlord to check up on a potential new tenant in the normal way. Consent cannot be unreasonably withheld and he must respond to your request within a reasonable period. If there is nothing prohibiting assigning or subletting in the agreement, the landlord can use the statutory prohibition included in the Housing Act 1988.

What happens at the end of the fixed term?

At the end of a fixed term, you can remain in possession as a statutory periodic tenant, but with

The websites **www.landlords.org.uk** and **www.rla.org.uk** offer tenancy agreements and forms that affect the tenancy as well as guidance. For further guidance on tenancy agreements, also go to **www.oft.gov.uk**.

no security of tenure, the landlord can evict you through possession proceedings (see pages 160–5). A shorthold that is a periodic tenancy can be terminated in the same way.

However, in both cases, the court cannot order the tenant out before six months have started since the grant of the tenancy, even if the fixed-term letting was for a shorter period, such as three months.

A landlord who wants to let for a period of less than six months and be sure of obtaining possession can only do so by granting an ordinary assured tenancy and using one of the ordinary assured mandatory grounds for possession (see pages 160–1).

'If you move out of a rented property before the end of the fixed term, the landlord can claim the full amount of rent that is due until the end of the period.'

Can I do whatever I like once the tenancy has been agreed?

Once a property is let, the law allows you to do more of less what you like with the premises. If the landlord wants to prevent a particular activity, it must be written into the agreement (see the sample clauses on pages 190–204).

Can I terminate a fixed-term agreement early?

The tenancy is a contract with obligations on both sides, so you can't sign a 12-month fixed-term agreement and expect to terminate it early without the landlord's consent. If you move out, the landlord can claim the full amount of rent that is due until the end of the fixed period.

You can terminate a periodic tenancy by serving notice in writing (a month for a monthly tenancy, four weeks for a weekly tenancy), unless the landlord agrees otherwise.

To complete a period of tenancy, under the 'corresponding day rule' the notice must expire on the same day of the week or month. So a weekly tenancy beginning on a Monday must terminate on a Monday (or technically midnight on Sunday), and a monthly tenancy commencing on the 23rd must expire on the 22nd or 23rd.

Social lets

Social lettings are those made by local authorities and some housing associations to tenants on Housing Benefit. As a private landlord you can apply to be a registered provider of social housing (see page 72).

The landlord's viewpoint

The questions in this section cover such subjects as means testing, the security of a local authority tenancy and the main responsibilities of a landlord with public-sector lets. If you are a tenant, this material may be of interest to you, too.

Is Housing Benefit means tested?

Housing Benefit, also known as rent rebate or rent allowance, is a means-tested payment to tenants who cannot pay their rent because they have no or a low income. It is administered by the relevant local authority, which is then reimbursed by central government. Payment of benefit is governed by the Housing Benefit regulations. From 2013 to 2017, Housing Benefit will be incorporated into Universal Credit.

If you rent from a private landlord, you may be able to claim additional benefits via the Local Housing Allowance (LHA) and/or Universal Credit as it takes into account the different rental costs by area. Payment is normally made to the tenant who should then pass it onto the landlord. Check the LHA by visiting the local authority website or the Rent Service's website (see below).

Are you affected by LHA caps?

The Coalition Government introduced caps on the amount of LHA from April 2011. If you are worried how this will affect you, speak to your local housing office, Citizens Advice or Shelter.

For the latest information on LHAs in your area visit www.voa.gov.uk/corporate/RentOfficers/localHousingAllowance.html.

What is a secure tenancy?

Properties let by local authorities and some housing associations have their own system of protection under the Housing Act 1985. If a tenancy is defined as a 'secure tenancy', the tenant has extensive security of tenure. There are also succession rights on their death and a 'right to buy' at a discount (see page 155–6). They were typically given before 1989 and you can't be given one as a new tenant.

To get information on Housing Benefit and Universal Credit, go to **www.gov.uk**, **www.dwp.gov.uk** and from your local council. See also **www.shelter.org.uk** and **www.adviceguide.org.uk**. The Rent Service LHA website is **https://lha-direct.voa.gov.uk/Secure/BedroomCalculator.aspx**.

A secure tenancy is a tenancy or licence of a house let as a separate dwelling at any time when both the 'landlord condition' and the 'tenant condition' are satisfied.

The landlord condition denotes that the interest of the landlord belongs to one of a specified list of bodies, including a local authority, a new town corporation, and an urban development corporation. A secure tenant is most likely to be a tenant of a district council.

The tenant condition denotes that the tenant is an individual occupying the house as his only or principal home. With joint tenants, only one needs to meet this requirement.

Unlike the definition of assured and protected tenancies, a social let expressly includes a licence to occupy. The licence can only amount to a secure tenancy if it confers the right to exclusive possession on the occupier; without it the tenant has no protection. Even when these two conditions are satisfied, there are exceptions where there will not be a secure tenancy.

Can a secure tenancy be assigned?

Secure tenancies cannot usually be passed to a new tenant and if a supposed assignment takes place, the tenancy is no longer secure. The exceptions are: as an exchange with another secure tenant; as part of a property adjustment order made in matrimonial proceedings, and to a person who, if the tenant died, would be entitled to succeed to the tenancy.

Can I end a security of tenure?

A landlord can only end a secure tenancy with a court order for possession. A notice to quit has no effect and when a fixed-term secure tenancy ends, it becomes a periodic secure tenancy. To obtain the court order for possession, the judge must follow a procedure and establish at least one of the grounds for possession laid down by the Act (see pages 170–1). There are no mandatory grounds, so there is no guarantee that possession will be ordered even if the ground is established.

Am I responsible for repairs to the property?

In the vast majority of cases, you are responsible for repairs to the structure and interior of the property and for keeping the facilities for the supply of gas and electricity, space and water heating and sanitation in repair and proper working order. The Secure Tenants of Local Housing Authorities (Right to Repair) Regulations 1994 give secure tenants the right to up to £50 in compensation if certain types of repair, to a maximum cost of £250, are not carried out within a prescribed period.

What happens on the death of a tenant?

The tenancy does not currently end with the death of a secure tenant: their spouse succeeds to it, subject to government changes provided they were still occupying the house as their only or principal home at the time of the death. The spouse is a person living with the tenant as husband or wife, including the survivor of an unmarried heterosexual couple.

If there is no 'spouse', a member of the tenant's family who has resided in the house with the tenant for at least 12 months prior to the death will succeed to the tenancy.

Only one succession is permitted, so there is no further succession after the death of a secure tenant who himself succeeded to it. In cases where there is no succession, the tenancy will pass on in the same way as the rest of the deceased's property, that is, either by their will or according to the rules of intestacy. However, it will no longer be a secure tenancy and you can take possession when it is terminated. This will take place under normal common law rules, for example, by notice to quit in the case of a periodic tenancy, and a court order will still be required.

How do I obtain a court order?

You must first give notice to the tenant in accordance with Section 83 of the Housing Act 1985 in the form laid down by the legislation, stating the particulars of the ground for possession with absolute clarity. If you fail to do the correct procedure, the tenant can claim that the notice is invalid.

If it is a periodic tenancy, as most council tenancies are, the notice must specify the earliest date on which possession proceedings can start, which cannot be earlier than the date on which you could have brought the tenancy to an end with a notice to quit. For a notice to be valid, as well as being of the correct length, it must expire on the day of the week or month corresponding to the one on which the tenancy began. So for a weekly tenancy commencing on Monday, the notice must expire on a Monday or a Sunday. With a monthly tenancy commencing on the 10th of the month, the notice must expire on the 9th or 10th of a subsequent month.

How do I set about obtaining possession?

Provided you follow the correct procedure (see page 160), the court must order possession. The notice must tell the tenant of his right to request a review challenging the landlord's decision to apply, which must be sought within 14 days of service of the notice. If requested, this review must be carried out and the tenant notified of the result before the date specified as the earliest on which the landlord could apply to the court. There is no further right of appeal.

Can anti-social behaviour be prohibited?

Under the Housing Act 1996, persons in secure or introductory tenancies can be prohibited from:

- **Engaging or threatening to engage** in conduct causing or likely to cause a nuisance or annoyance to a person residing in or visiting or nearby the premises.

- **Using or threatening to use the premises** for immoral or illegal purposes.
- **Entering such premises** or being found in the vicinity of such premises.

The local authority and registered providers of social housing can apply to the county court for an order only if the person in question has used or threatened violence and there is a significant risk of harm if the injunction is not granted. If the order is obtained, the person can be arrested if they breach the injunction.

Does a demoted tenancy relate to anti-social behaviour too?

The demoted tenancy is a one-year council probationary tenancy introduced as a means to help prevent anti-social behaviour. Local authorities and registered social landlords can apply to the county court to ask for a secure or assured tenancy to be amended to a demoted tenancy for a period of 12 months. If a demotion order is made, then during the 12-month period the landlord may obtain an order for possession without establishing a ground for possession. If the demoted tenant doesn't break their tenancy agreement, they should become secure tenants again after 12 months.

The effect on the tenant depends on whether the tenant is a secure or assured tenant. If the court decides to grant a demotion order, this will end the secure tenancy and be replaced by a demoted tenancy. An assured tenant of a registered provider of social housing will find their tenancy is relegated to a demoted assured shorthold tenancy. Any tenant who comes within either a demoted tenancy or demoted assured shorthold tenancy will lose a number of rights enjoyed under their previous tenancy, for example, the right to buy their home (see pages 155–6).

If you want to seek a demotion order, you must serve a notice and then proceedings for the court. Check the type of tenancy agreement your tenant may have, whether it is secure or assured, as there are different requirements when serving the notice. If you have a secure tenant, you must serve a notice that is in a prescribed form giving particulars of the grounds that you are relying on. If the tenancy is assured, the notice is not prescribed so there is no standard form for it.

The grounds for possession are limited to anti-social behaviour grounds. The court will only make an order if the tenant, someone else living in the property or a visitor to the tenant's home has behaved or threatened to behave in a way which is capable of causing nuisance or annoyance. The court must also be satisfied that it is reasonable to make the order. If you want to pursue this step, take advice from your legal representative.

The tenant's take

The questions in this section cover key areas ranging from tenancy agreements and rent levels through to problems with the property you live in and rights that you may have to buy your own home one day.

Is there anything I should be aware of in the agreement?

The use of the phrase 'at any time when' indicates that the status of the tenancy can change during its term, depending on whether the landlord condition and the tenant condition (see page 150) are satisfied. Security is lost if either condition ceases to apply. There is no requirement for rent to be paid, nor exemption for low-rental tenancies. If you are ever in doubt about your agreement or have any queries, consult a legal representative before signing it.

What is an introductory tenancy?

The Housing Act 1996 allowed local housing authorities to elect to set up an introductory tenancy scheme. When such an election is in place, any periodic tenancy or licence that would otherwise be a secure tenancy will instead be an introductory tenancy: a one-year trial period before being given security of tenure. This cannot be applied to a tenant who already has a secure tenancy, even if it was for a different house or not granted by the local authority.

If you then prove suitable, your tenancy automatically becomes a secure one. If you don't, the local authority can obtain possession without having to prove the usual secure tenancy grounds. A court order will still be required and proceedings must be commenced during the trial period.

What rent control is there?

For secure tenancies, rents are fixed by the local authority, so you can't control the amount of rent paid, but you can claim Housing Benefit (or, from 2013,Universal Credit) to help. However, if you have a tenancy that started before 15 January 1989 and you are a housing association or

The website for the Housing Ombudsman Service (HOS) is at **www.housing-ombudsman.org.uk**. Although the service is mainly aimed at landlords, there is nevertheless plenty of advice for tenants, too. Read also pages 150-3.

housing co-operative tenant, your rent is likely to have been registered and assessed by the rent officer. The rent then won't be changed for two years from the start of the tenancy.

Can I make improvements to the property?

An implied term of every secure tenancy is that you can't undertake any improvement, alteration or addition to the property without the landlord's consent. This cannot be unreasonably withheld and if it is, you can proceed anyway. Technically, consent is required for installing a satellite dish or TV aerial, although such an act is unlikely to be accepted as grounds for possession.

Can I complain about my accommodation?

Tenants of registered social landlords can complain direct to the Housing Ombudsman Service. The ombudsman has wide powers to order the landlord to pay compensation, to alter contracts and to publicise poor practice.

Local authority tenants who are unhappy with the service they receive can complain to the authority's housing department or talk to their local councillor. They can also go to the local government ombudsman.

Can I sublet or take in a lodger?

There is a clamp down on secure tenants subletting or taking in a lodger, so if you want to do this, you must have written permission from your landlord.

Can I end a security of tenure?

Yes, a tenant can end a periodic tenancy with the usual notice to quit – see page 151.

What should I do if I receive a court order?

If you receive a notice of intention to start possession proceedings, you will not get a notice to quit as well: the next step the landlord can take is to begin court proceedings. These must commence within 12 months, but if ground 2 (see page 170) is being alleged, the landlord can start possession proceedings as soon as the notice has been served.

Might I have a right to buy?

The right to buy gives secure tenants the option to buy the freehold of a house or a 125-year lease on a flat, and has proved very popular since its introduction in 1980. The rules that determine whether you are eligible for the right to buy are complicated. Secure tenants and assured tenants who used to be secure can apply.

The discount depends on how long you have been a public-sector tenant, whether the property is a house or a flat (which get a higher discount), and the age and condition of the property. It is calculated as a percentage of the value of the property but

Suspension of right to buy

A local authority landlord is entitled to apply to court for a suspension order providing that a right to buy may not be exercised in relation to a property. A court will not make a suspension order unless it is satisfied that the tenant or a person living or visiting the premises, engaged or threatened to engage in anti-social behaviour or used the premises for unlawful purposes. The court must also consider that it is reasonable to make an order.

there is a maximum discount for properties in different areas of the country. You can get up to a maximum of a £75,000 discount. For more information, go to www.communities.gov.uk and read their 'Your right to buy your home' leaflet.

You have the right to buy if you live in a housing association property and, under the Housing Act 1996, most tenants of registered provider of social housing have the right to buy their homes on the same terms as council tenants, provided the property was built or purchased with public money and has remained in the social rented sector. Secure tenants with a local authority may have the right to buy their own home, too. In the case of demoted tenancies (see page 153), different rules apply – seek advice.

If you buy a leasehold property, you may be liable to repair costs that could amount to thousands of pounds. So before going ahead with such a purchase, check this possibility with your legal company and seek specialist advice from www.lease-advice.org.

How do I apply for the right to buy?

Contact your landlord and request the right-to-buy claim form (RTB1). Complete and return the form, keeping a copy. The landlord has to provide a decision within four to eight weeks. It must give a reason for any refusal, and you can ask for a more detailed explanation. Contact a local advice centre if you are in this situation.

BE CAREFUL!

If you decide to sell your home within the first five years, or it is repossessed by your mortgage lender during that time, you will have to repay some or all of the right-to-buy discount.

The grounds for possession relating to a public-sector tenancy are given on pages 170–1. Taking legal action is described on pages 160–1 and 167.

Legal action

10

Letting is a business, and disputes can occur, as in any other trade. This chapter explains the rights and responsibilities that tenants and landlords need to respect, and describes what you need to do if you have to start legal proceedings. In all cases, it is important to seek professional legal advice prior to taking any action.

Avoiding legal action

Start out on the right track and you are less likely to reach the position where legal action has to be taken. It is important that the rights and obligations of the landlord and tenant are clear in the tenancy agreement.

In the main, most tenants have a good renting experience and most landlords enjoy letting their properties. There are times, though, when things just go wrong. Sometimes these are due to human error or just bad luck and in these cases, the best thing to do as a landlord or tenant is find a compromise that you can both live with that brings any disagreements to a swift close.

There are times too when as a landlord or as a tenant you are deliberately targeted and have to take legal action to put the situation right, but this should always be a last resort.

BE CAREFUL!

When creating a contract, you need to be aware of the Office of Fair Trading (OFT) guidance on unfair terms in tenancy agreements. This states that landlords and agents deal fairly with tenants and not balance tenancy terms so much in the landlord's favour that it affects the tenant's legal rights.

To help avoid legal action on both sides and find ways of swiftly resolving situations, both landlords and tenants need to understand what their individual responsibilties are.

As a landlord

A landlord is generally responsible for the following:

- Providing an EPC when marketing the property.
- Any obligations that are agreed within the terms of the tenancy agreement.
- General property repairs.
- Fire safety.
- Fixtures and fittings, such as baths, sinks, basins and other sanitaryware.
- Heating and hot water installations.
- The structure and exterior of the property (if the property is a flat, then other parts of the building or installations that the landlord owns and/or controls).

For more advice, see also 'Entering into a contract' on pages 79–87 and 108–10, 'Managing the let' on pages 88–90 and 'A tenant's obligations' on pages 111–14.

- Complying with legal regulations, such as gas and electrical safety regulations.
- Protecting the tenant's deposit in an independent scheme.
- Securing any licences required by the local authority, for example for licensed HMOs.

The landlord can also expect to have the property handed back in the same condition and with the same items in it as at the start of the let.

As a tenant

A tenant has the following rights:

- To understand when searching for a property how much it would cost to heat the home and how energy efficient it is via an EPC.
- To rent a property that is safe to live in and with tested utilities.
- To be allowed to live in the property without being harassed by the landlord who is not able to enter the premises without the tenant's permission unless in an emergency.
- To have things repaired in a reasonable time frame.
- To have their deposit returned in a timely manner.

What if the agreement isn't being followed?

There are various ways of dealing with disputes, which are covered by the tenancy agreement.

First, whether you are a landlord or a tenant, you need to understand what it is that the other party is doing, has done or hasn't done and whether it has broken the agreement in some way. If you have a good relationship with each other, or with the agent, make a phone call or meet them to talk through the problem and what you would like to happen next. Make a note of the date, time and detail of the discussion, what was agreed and when things were agreed to be done by. If you can, also discuss what happens if the matter is not resolved as agreed.

If it's not possible to meet or nothing happens after the meeting or call, then you need to write to the other party, explaining what has happened (or not) and what needs to happen next. If you have to post a letter, do it via recorded delivery or if it's by email, ask for a 'read receipt'.

If there continues to be a problem, then you need to seek specialist advice. Go to Citizens Advice, Shelter, www.propertychecklists.co.uk or a legal company and then write again (as above) and explain what will happen if nothing is done.

If the problem is still not solved, as a landlord you need to decide whether it warrants taking steps towards eviction. If you are a tenant, you need to consider (and seek legal advice) whether you withhold some or part of your rent, or take steps to report the landlord/letting agent to a trade association, ombudsman or local housing officer.

If you rented/let the property through a council scheme or accommodation office, discuss with them what else you can do to resolve the problem.

Obtaining a court order

In most cases, a landlord needs to obtain a court order for regaining possession. The way to set about doing this varies, depending on your agreement.

To obtain a court order, you need to be able to:

- Show that the tenancy has ended and that you have issued the appropriate termination notices.
- Prove there are grounds for possession.
- Show it is reasonable for the court to grant possession if the ground is discretionary rather than mandatory.

Following the grounds for possession (see right), information for each type of tenancy is given on pages 163–7.

BE CAREFUL!

If the landlord resorts to obtaining possession without a court order, this will normally amount to unlawful eviction, for which an injunction may be taken out against the landlord. If this is successful, he may be ordered to pay substantial damages, a fine or, in extreme cases, may even be sent to prison.

Grounds for possession

There are 17 grounds for possession relating to assured tenancies, all discretionary to some degree – they are described on pages 168–9. In addition, there are grounds for possession relating to public-sector tenancies, which are described on pages 170–1. At any time, it is important to gain independent legal advice for possession as it is a complicated matter and the legals may have changed once this book has been published.

Notice periods

You must serve a notice seeking possession of the property on the tenant before you start court proceedings. You must give the following amount of notice:

- **For grounds 3, 4, 8, 10, 11, 12, 13, 15 or 17:** at least two weeks.
- **For grounds 1, 2, 5, 6, 7, 9, and 16:** at lease two months. If the tenancy is on a contractual periodic or statutory periodic basis, the notice period must end on the last day of a tenancy period. The notice period must

also be at least as long as the period of the tenancy, so that three months' notice must be given if it is a quarterly tenancy.

- **For ground 14:** you can start proceedings as soon as you have served a notice.

Grounds 1 to 5 (see page 168): These are grounds where you have to provide prior notice, which means these can usually only be used once you have notified the tenants in writing before the tenancy started that you always intended to ask for the property back on one of those grounds.

The court may give possession on grounds 1 or 2 if prior notice has not been given if the court considers there are reasons for not serving the notice. If you also have grounds for possession, then you have to give written notice to the tenant that you intend to go to court to seek possession. The period of the notice can be between two weeks and two months, depending on the ground that has been used. The notice must be given on a form (see box, right) required under Section 8 of the Housing Act 1988. This is called a 'notice seeking possession for property let under an assured tenancy or an assured agricultural occupancy'. This notice is available from law stationers and rent assessment panel offices.

The tenant should leave the property on the date that is specified in the court order. If this doesn't happen and the tenant refuses to leave, you cannot evict the tenant yourself as a claim could be made against you for unlawful harassment. You must apply for a warrant for possession from the court. The court will arrange for bailiffs to evict the tenant.

If a mandatory ground is used and the court orders possession, the tenant will have to leave on the date specified in the court order.

If a discretionary ground is used, the court has the discretion to either grant a final possession order or may allow the tenant to stay on at the property with a suspended possession order. The terms for allowance of the tenant to stay on in the property would be to pay back an amount of rent arrears each week or to abide by the terms of the tenancy if possession was sought on anti-social behaviour. If a suspended possession order is made, the tenant cannot be evicted, provided the tenant meets the conditions.

If a tenant breaches the terms of a suspended possession order, then you are able to apply to the court for a final possession order.

BE CAREFUL!

The forms for court orders are described in the Housing Act 1988. If you deviate from the format, you run the risk that the notice will be found to be defective. Although rare, there is provision for the court to suspend service of the notice if it is unreasonable. So check these forms with a specialist legal adviser.

Occasions when you do not need a court order to obtain possession

The exceptional cases in which a court order is not needed are called 'excluded licences or tenancies'. These include resident landlords where the following conditions exist:

- The landlord/licensor occupied the property as his only or main residence before the tenancy/licence began, and under its terms the occupier now shares accommodation with them; or

- The occupier shares accommodation with one or more of the landlord's family and the following conditions also apply:

  a) The landlord/licensor's main home is in the same building (unless it is a purpose-built block of flats)

  b) A member of the landlord/licensor's family shares accommodation with the tenant-licensee.

Other excluded tenancies/licenses are:

- Holiday lets, where the occupier fails to vacate
- Gratuitous lettings, where the accommodation is made available rent-free
- Squatters and trespassers, where the agreement was given as a temporary measure
- Hostels, where the accommodation is a residential hostel.

In all other cases a court order is essential

- In any of these cases, you may still need to gain possession by obtaining a court order but a notice to quit may not need to be served under the Protection From Eviction Act 1977 and the occupant will not have any defence to a possession claim.
- No unreasonable force can be used to evict an occupant.

Which step you take depends on the terms of the order that was made by the court.

Assured shorthold tenancies

If the tenancy has expired and you do not wish to renew it, or if it is a periodic assured shorthold tenancy and you wish to terminate it and not grant a new tenancy to the same tenant, the procedure is:

- **Give at least two months' notice** under Section 21 of the 1988 Act (known as 'Section 21 notice' – see box, right) requiring possession when the notice expires.
- **If the tenant does not move out** as a result of the notification, you will have to go to court to seek a possession order. The court cannot make a possession order in the first six months of the tenancy. You must take legal advice at this point.
- **You do not need to issue a ground for possession** for an assured shorthold tenancy and there is an 'accelerated possession action' (see overleaf).
- **You also do not need to show** that granting possession is reasonable.

If the tenancy was granted initially for more than six months, the notice cannot take effect before the fixed term expires. So if the tenancy was granted for 12 months, the notice is not effective until the end of that period. If you seek possession before it expires or during the first six months, it must be based on a ground for possession (see pages 168–9).

BE CAREFUL!

Sometimes a tenant will not answer the door and so cannot have notice served on them. Take a witness and put the notice through the letterbox before 5pm. It is then deemed to have been served on the following day.

Section 21 notice

The precise form of this notice can vary, but it must be in writing and must specify the date of required possession, which cannot be sooner than two months after notice is served. You can obtain printed forms from law stationers or (in some cases free) from www.rla.org.uk, www.clickdocs.co.uk, www.landlordlaw.co.uk and www.landlordzone.co.uk.

The specified date cannot be earlier than the end of the fixed term, and if the fixed term has expired or tenancy was periodic, the date specified must be the last day of a rental period. So for a monthly tenancy with a rent day on the 15th of the month, the date specified will be the 14th of a month at least two months after the date of service. As the two-month notice period is a minimum, there is nothing to stop you issuing a Section 21 notice early in the tenancy, to take effect at the end of that six months' let.

Tenant's take

If you receive an application for accelerated possession, you are likely to have to leave the property by the specified date. The court is not allowed to consider whether this is fair or reasonable provided you have an assured shorthold tenancy. A defence form is sent with the application and you have 14 days in which to return it if you wish. If you think there are reasons why the court should not make a possession order, get advice from a solicitor, advice agency or local council. You may qualify for assistance from the Community Legal Service Fund. More information is available from Citizens Advice, Shelter and www.communitylegaladvice.org.uk.

Accelerated possession

This is a quicker way to gain possession of your property as there is no court hearing. However, take independent legal advice on any type of possession.

- **Find the county court** for the area where the property is situated, then fill in form N5B claim for possession (accelerated procedure), obtainable from HM Courts & Tribunals Service.
- **You will also need to supply:**
  - A copy of the tenancy agreement.
  - If the tenancy began before 28 February 1997, the notice stating that the tenancy would be an assured shorthold.
  - The notice requiring possession served under Section 21 of the Housing Act 1988.
  - A copy of the form and witness statement for each defendant.
- **You will need to pay a fee** before the action can commence.

The court posts the papers to the tenants with a form of reply allowing them to lodge an objection within 14 days if they wish to. The district judge checks the papers and any reply from the tenants and orders possession or, if the paperwork is not in order or the tenant has raised a legitimate issue, refers the matter for a hearing. If the court is satisfied that all is in order and there is no defence, it notifies tenant and landlord of the order for possession.

Ordinary assured tenancies

If you are trying to get possession on grounds 1, 3, 4 or 5 (see page 168), you can use the accelerated possession action (see left) but otherwise (for instance, if you are also claiming for rent arrears), use the ordinary possession action on page 163.

BE CAREFUL!

This procedure only deals with possession claims and for the costs of making the application. Claims for rent arrears are covered by an ordinary possession action (see page 160).

Ending the tenancy

First, issue a 'claim form for possession of property' and a 'particulars of claim (rented residential premises)' form, both downloadable from www.justice.gov.uk/about/hmcts.

The completed form is filed at the local county court for the area where the property is situated, together with a copy for each tenant and the court fee. The court serves these forms and notifies both parties of the hearing date. The tenant can file a defence or reply if he or she is going to dispute the claim for possession.

The matter is listed before either a district judge or a circuit judge and both parties can give evidence. The judge must be satisfied that you have made your case, that the tenant has no defence and, if you are relying on a discretionary ground for possession, that a possession order is reasonable.

The standard procedure

This is slow but effective. If you are lucky, the defaulting tenant will move on receipt of a court summons, but he or she may wait until a judgement is given or for the bailiffs to arrive. The process can take three to five months. The speed with which a case is heard is decided by factors such as the amount of arrears and the importance given to the defendant or the landlord keeping or regaining possession. Be aware that the Government spending cuts may mean there are a reduced number of courts, so cases may take longer.

- **Notice of proceedings** takes at least two weeks.
- **It takes an average two months** to get a hearing date.
- **A possession order** can be up to six weeks from the date of the hearing.

If the tenant doesn't leave, apply for an eviction appointment with a county court bailiff. It could take up to six weeks to get an appointment. Given this timescale, some landlords offer the tenant a month's free rent on condition that they move out. The loss of rental income is balanced by the opportunity to start re-letting the property when the month is over.

Online procedure

Rent possession proceedings can be issued online. The court issue fee is £50 cheaper than for a paper application and the progress of the case can be tracked online. The final hearing takes place at the county court.

To find the nearest county court, go to **www.justice.gov.uk/about/hmcts/** or telephone 020 7189 2000 or 0845 456 8770.

Assured tenancies

These tenancies give the tenant full security of tenure under the Housing Act 1988. This section also applies to assured shorthold tenancies if the landlord seeks possession before the end of the fixed term.

Ending the tenancy

- **You must serve notice** under Section 8 of the Housing Act. There is a set format for this form, which can be bought at law stationers or downloaded for a fee from sites, such as www.rla.org.uk, and other sites including www.clickdocs.co.uk and www.landlordlaw.co.uk.

Protected and statutory tenancies

These tenancies created by the Rent Act 1977 offer great security to tenants, making it very hard for the landlord to get vacant possession.

Ending the tenancy

- **If the tenancy is periodic, you must serve a notice to quit,** properly known as notice requiring repossession, containing the information stipulated by the Protection from Eviction Act 1977 and the regulations made under that Act.
- **The eviction date** must be at least four weeks after the notice and must bring the tenancy to an end at the close of a complete period of the tenancy (for example, at the end of a month, if the tenancy is by the month).
- **It must also include the information that** if the tenant or licensee does not leave the dwelling, the landlord or licensor must get an order for possession from the court before the tenant or licensee can lawfully be evicted. The landlord or licensor cannot apply for such an order before the notice to quit or notice to determine has run out.

The form will be provided by your legal company or can be purchased from a law stationer or downloaded from www.clickdocs.co.uk and www.letlink.co.uk.

Grounds for possession

The landlord has to prove a ground for possession, which does not have to be specified in the notice to quit but will be pleaded in the court action. Some grounds are mandatory, others are not, but it is worth pointing out that rent arrears are always discretionary grounds in Rent Act cases, however large the sum, in contrast to those in assured and assured shorthold tenancies where serious arrears are mandatory grounds. The grounds are described on pages 168–9.

Reasonableness

If the ground stated is discretionary, the court will decide if it is reasonable to grant the order for possession. In rent arrears cases, it is common for the order to be suspended if the tenant pays the correct rent and an agreed amount with each payment to cover the arrears.

Public-sector tenancies

If the landlord is a local authority, the Housing Act 1985 applies, but if it is a housing association and the tenancy was granted on or after 15 January 1989, the rules on assured and assured shorthold tenancies normally apply. So this advice relates only to council houses and flats.

Ending the tenancy

- **The authority or landlord** must serve a notice seeking possession in a prescribed form, giving at least four weeks' notice of intention to commence proceedings. The actual notice period is decided by when the rent is payable. For example, if it is a monthly rent, one calendar month's notice is needed. Notice is valid for 12 months, during which period the landlord can start proceedings at any time.

Grounds for possession

Unless it is an 'introductory tenancy' (see page 154), you will have to specify and prove a ground for possession (see pages 170–1). The court cannot make an order for possession on grounds 1–8 unless it considers it reasonable to do so. It can only agree to possession on grounds 9–11 if it is satisfied that suitable alternative accommodation will be available to the tenant when the order takes effect. Grounds 12–16 must be considered reasonable and, again, only if alternative accommodation is available.

Reasonableness

If the ground is discretionary (which includes rent arrears), the court decides if it is reasonable to grant possession.

In cases of rent arrears, the court often suspends the order if the tenant pays the correct rent and an agreed amount with each payment to cover the arrears.

Other tenancies

Some tenancies, such as where the landlord is resident, are not covered by the rules explained in this chapter, and offer no security of tenure. However, you, as landlord, will still need to show the tenancy has come to an end, or the licence to occupy has been terminated. An ordinary possession action in the local county court is subsequently required, with a hearing before a judge.

Ending the tenancy

- **If the tenancy/licence was for a fixed term,** no notice is required and possession proceedings can start as soon as the term ends.
- **If it is periodic,** you must give 'reasonable notice', which may be specified in the agreement or is otherwise generally agreed to be four weeks.

Grounds for possession

None are required.

Reasonableness

Not required.

Grounds for possession: assured tenancy

A tenant has to break one of these grounds before a court order can be obtained, as described on pages 160-1.

Mandatory grounds on which the court must order possession

Ground 1:
A prior notice ground
You used to live in the property as your main home. Or, so long as you or someone before you did when the tenancy started, you or your spouse require it to be lived in as your main home.

Ground 2:
A prior notice ground
The property is subject to a mortgage which was granted before the tenancy started and the lender, usually a bank or building society, wants to sell it, normally to pay off arrears.

Ground 3:
A prior notice ground
The tenancy is for a fixed term of not more than eight months and that at some time during the 12 months before the tenancy started, the property was let for a holiday.

Ground 4:
A prior notice ground
The tenancy is for a fixed term of not more than 12 months and at some time during the 12 months before the tenancy started, the property was let to students by an educational establishment, such as a university or college.

Ground 5:
A prior notice ground
The property is held for use for a minister of religion and is now needed for that particular purpose.

Ground 6
You intend to substantially redevelop the property and cannot do so with the tenant there. The ground cannot be used where you, or someone before you, bought the property with an existing tenant, or where the work could be carried out without the tenant having to move. The tenant's removal expenses will have to be paid.

Ground 7
The former tenant, who must have had a contractual periodic tenancy or statutory periodic tenancy, has died in the 12 months before possession proceedings started and there is no one living there who has a right to succeed to the tenancy.

Ground 8
The tenant owed at lease two months' rent if the tenancy is on a monthly basis or eight weeks' rent if it is on a weekly basis, both when you gave notice seeking possession and at the date of the court hearing.

Note: This ground was amended by the Housing Act 1996 and applied from 28 February 1997.

Discretionary grounds on which the court may order possession

Ground 9
Suitable alternative accommodation is available for the tenant, or will be when the court order takes effect. The tenant's removal expenses will have to be paid.

Ground 10
The tenant was behind with his or her rent both when you served the notice seeking possession and when you began court proceedings.

Ground 11
Even if the tenant was not behind with his or her rent when you started possession proceedings, he or she has been persistently late paying the rent.

Ground 12
The tenant has broken one or more of the terms of the tenancy agreement, except the obligation to pay rent.

Ground 13
The condition of the property has got worse because of the behaviour of the tenant or any other person living there.

Ground 14
The tenant or someone living in or visiting the property who:

- Has caused, or is likely to cause, a nuisance or annoyance to someone living in or visiting the locality; or
- Has been convicted of using the property, or allowing it to be used, for immoral or illegal purposes, or an arrestable offence committed in the property or in the locality.

  Note: This ground was amended by the Housing Act 1996 and applies from 28 February 1997.

Ground 15
The condition of the furniture in the property has got worse because it has been ill treated by the tenant or any other person living there.

Ground 16
The tenancy was granted because the tenant was employed by you, or a former landlord, but he or she is no longer employed by you.

Ground 17
You were persuaded to grant the tenancy on the basis of a false statement knowingly or recklessly made by the tenant, or a person acting at the tenant's instigation.

Note: This is a new ground added by the Housing Act 1996 and applies from 28 February 1997.

Grounds for possession: a public-sector tenancy

Ground 1
Rent lawfully due has not been paid or some other obligation under the tenancy has not been complied with. There is no minimum amount of rent which must be due before this ground is used, but the court takes into account the amount and frequency of the arrears in deciding if it is reasonable. Landlords, including those who are local authorities, must provide their tenants with an address in England or Wales at which documents can be served on them in order for the rent to be lawfully due.

Ground 2
The behaviour of the tenant or someone at the house (even a visitor) is or is likely to cause annoyance or nuisance to others in the neighbourhood, or they have been convicted of using the house for an illegal or immoral purpose or of an arrestable offence committed in the locality. This ground is identical to assured tenancy ground 14 (see page 169) and has been used by some authorities to 'clean up' housing estates.

Ground 2A
Intended to provide help to victims of domestic violence, this ground applies where the house was occupied by a couple (not necessarily married or of different sex) but the tenancy was in only one of their names. It allows for possession if one of the occupants has had to leave the house due to violence or the threat of it by the other and it is unlikely that they will return. It does not matter if they are not the tenant: the landlord can gain possession against the violent partner and thus provide a safe home for the victim.

Ground 3
The condition of the house has deteriorated due to the acts or neglect of the tenant or another resident. If it was the latter, it must be shown that the tenant has not taken reasonable steps to try to remove the other person.

Ground 4
The same as ground 3, but relating to the condition of the furniture provided by the landlord.

Ground 5
The landlord granted the tenancy due to a false statement by the tenant or their representative. This is the same as assured tenancy ground 17 (see page 169).

Ground 6
The tenancy was assigned to the tenant and a premium was paid in connection with this assignment. Secure tenancies cannot usually be assigned at all. If an unlawful assignment is made, the tenancy is no longer secure and the landlord can take possession without proving a ground.

Ground 7
The house is part of a building that is used mainly for non-housing purposes and the house was let to the tenant by reason of his employment and the tenant or a co-resident has behaved in a way that it would not be right for him to stay in the house, given the purpose for which the building is used.

Ground 8
The house was made available while the tenant's previous property was being repaired and this house is now ready.

Ground 9
The house is so overcrowded it is an offence under the Housing Act 1985. The definition of overcrowding is complex, but includes situations such as two or more people of different sexes over the age of 10 sharing a room, unless they are living together as man and wife.

Ground 10
The landlords intend to demolish or reconstruct the house and cannot reasonably do so without having obtained possession.

Ground 10A
The house is within the area of a redevelopment scheme approved by the Secretary of State or the Housing Corporation and the landlord intends to dispose of it in accordance with the scheme.

Ground 11
The landlord is a charity and the tenant's continued occupation of the house would conflict with the aims and objectives of the charity.

Ground 12
The house forms part of a building that is used mainly for non-housing purposes, was let to the tenant by reason of his employment, and is now required for occupation by another person in the landlord's employment.

Ground 13
The house has features designed to make it suitable for physically disabled persons, is no longer occupied by sucha person, and the landlord requires possession to allow a disabled person to live in it.

Ground 14
The landlord is a housing association or trust which lets property to persons whose circumstances (other than financial) make it difficult for them to get housing, is no longer occupied by such a person, and possession is required for occupation by such a person.

Ground 15
The house is one of a group of houses let for occupation by persons with special needs, is no longer occupied by such a person, and possession is required for occupation by such a person.

Ground 16
The accommodation is more extensive than is reasonably required by the tenant and the tenancy vested in the tenant on the death of the previous tenant, who was not his spouse, and the notice of proceedings for possession was served between 6 and 12 months after the date of the previous tenant's death.

Hearing a possession action

The hearing of a possession action is normally held before a district judge, and you should attend to give evidence and the tenant is also obviously entitled to attend as well.

If you are relying on discretionary grounds (see pages 161 and 169), the judge will decide if they are sufficient to make an order of poession. The different types of order are defined as follows.

'Absolute order for possession and postponed order for possession are the two legal steps that a judge could use after hearing a case.'

Order against the landlord

If you fail to make out a claim for possession, perhaps by not serving the appropriate notices properly, your proceedings may be dismissed. The tenant can then apply for an order for costs against you, and if the tenant succeeds in a counterclaim against you, he can claim damages.

- **Absolute order for possession.** This specifies a date 14 days (for possession on mandatory grounds) after the hearing when the tenant must leave the property, unless they will suffer exceptional hardship, in which case the date is postponed by up to 42 days. When grounds are discretionary, the normal period is 28 days.
- **Postponed order for possession.** These are used frequently in rent arrears cases. The court may decide to suspend the order if the tenant complies with obligations, typically paying off the arrears by instalments. If the tenant defaults on these terms, you can return to court to make the postponed order final.

Adjournment

When you are relying on discretionary grounds, the

See pages 169 to remind yourself of which grounds are more discretionary than others! There are strict laws laid down for which grounds the court has more leeway on than others.

court may decide not to make a possession order at all, but adjourn to a later date or indefinitely subject to certain terms and conditions. Typical terms would be for the tenant to pay off the arrears by a certain amount each week or month. An adjournment is rather like a postponed order, except that the landlord has to re-apply for a possession order if the tenant breaks the set terms.

Adjournment

When you are relying on discretionary grounds, the court may decide not to make a possession order at all, but adjourn to a later date or indefinitely subject to certain terms and conditions. Typical terms would be for the tenant to pay off the arrears by a certain amount each week or month. An adjournment is rather like a postponed order, except that the landlord has to re-apply for a possession order if the tenant breaks the set terms.

Legal costs

The court decides who should pay the legal costs incurred by the case. The successful party can make an application for costs as appropriate, and the court will then decide how much the losing party should pay.

Enforcement of possession orders

If the tenant does not vacate by the date specified, the order must be enforced by the court bailiff. The landlord must apply for a 'warrant for possession' and the bailiff will carry out the eviction.

'The court can hand down an absolute order for possession or a suspended order for possession, depending on the circumstances.'

Harassment

Sadly, some landlords resort to making life hell for their tenants by disrupting their lives, making threats or using violence as a cheaper, easier, quicker method of eviction. It is against the law and there are remedies tenants can pursue.

Here are some examples of unacceptable behaviour by landlords:

- Locking the tenant out, or preventing them from getting into part of the accommodation.
- Interfering with the gas, electricity or water supplies.
- Interfering with or confiscating tenant's possessions.
- Removing doors or windows.
- Persistently disturbing the tenant.
- Refusing to allow friends to visit.
- Moving in to part of the accommodation.
- Insisting that you hand over the keys.
- Using threats.
- Making abusive phone calls.
- Throwing out the tenant.

It is also possible for a tenant to harass a landlord and a landlord then has the right to go to law, too.

Get advice

People who may be able to help mediate or advise in disputes include:

- Most councils have a tenancy relations service or other staff who work in this field.
- Large institutions with accommodation offices usually have staff trained to help in this field.
- Students can consult their Student Union.
- Citizens Advice or Shelter.
- If you believe an offence is being committed, call the police.

If a dispute is developing, get advice as soon as you can to try to stop the conflict escalating.

Dealing with harassment

As a tenant, never respond physically or abusively or withhold rent: tell your landlord in person or (better) in writing that they are disturbing your peaceful occupation of the property. If possible, have someone with you as a witness whenever you are speaking with the landlord. Keep dated notes of any relevant incidents.

The landlord should give 'reasonable' notice (which is generally 24 hours) if he or she wants to visit the property, and you are entitled to refuse entry if this is not given – this also gives you time to ensure a witness will be present. A landlord should never let himself into the property, and entering it without permission is trespassing. If you feel threatened, you could add a security chain to the front door or change the locks, and you can also inform the police. If you are locked out, keep any keys you have as evidence.

Most disputes originate from simple misunderstandings that are allowed to escalate, and the majority of disputes can be settled early on through improved communication, sometimes with the help of a mediator. However, if things do get out of hand, tenants who receive poor treatment from their landlords may have civil remedies as well as criminal sanctions available to them. The basic remedies are damages, either compensation for loss suffered, or an injunction ordering the landlord to stop the behaviour.

Criminal sanctions

If you are dealing with harrassment, there are various legal sanctions designed to help you.

The Protection from Eviction Act 1977

This Act imposes criminal penalties for harassment and unlawful eviction, and proceedings are normally brought by the local authority (although private prosecutions are possible).

Protection from eviction

A residential occupier (which includes all tenants and licensees, whatever their statutory protection) cannot be evicted without a court order unless the landlord reasonably believes he no longer lives on the premises.

Contact the landlord

It is usually preferable to settle a matter out of court and it is possible the landlord did not realise his actions were unlawful. If at all possible, you or your solicitor should contact the landlord or letting agent, even if only by telephone, and explain the problem. The matter may be resolved at this stage, and if not, the record of this contact can form part of the evidence on the landlord's conduct.

Protection from harassment

There are two offences of harassment:

- **Section 1(3) harassment** is an act likely to interfere with the peace or comfort of a residential occupier or to withhold services reasonably required for occupation with intent to cause the occupier to leave. Proving 'intent' may be difficult, but it can be presumed if the actions had a foreseeable result: removing the doors makes it very difficult for the occupier to remain on the property!
- **Section 1(3A) harassment** covers similarly defined acts that the landlord knows or has reasonable cause to believe will cause the occupier to leave. Because of the absence of the need to show 'intent' this offence is easier to prove.

The Criminal Law Act 1977

The police are responsible for prosecutions under this Act in which Section 6(2) states it is an offence for anyone 'without lawful authority' to use or threaten to use violence to enter premises if there is someone there at the time who is opposed to the entry. Again, it is possible to prosecute privately.

Compensation in criminal proceedings

Section 35 of the Powers of the Criminal Courts Act 1973 gives magistrates the power to order compensation for personal injury, loss or damage resulting from an offence. This provides an easy, cost-free method for a tenant to obtain compensation, but magistrates' courts tend to award less than civil courts would, and are not empowered to order a landlord to restore a dispossessed tenant to a property.

Civil proceedings

Criminal proceedings punish bad behaviour but are not always the best option for a dispossessed or threatened occupier who is more likely to want to claim for damages or obtain an injunction to stop the landlord's behaviour or to regain possession of the property. You have to go through civil proceedings in the county court.

Get a solicitor

It is possible to bring proceedings for harassment or unlawful eviction on a 'self-help' basis, but speed and accuracy are essential and, if possible, it makes sense to get professional help from a solicitor who has experience in landlord/tenant litigation. If you qualify for public funding, a solicitor can be instructed at little or no cost. If not, you can get assistance from law centres, housing advice centres, the local authority tenancy relations office, Citizens Advice or Shelter.

Injunctions

Injunctions aim to prevent the problem recurring. An occupier who has been awarded damages will still want protection and reassurance that the harassment won't happen again. Injunctions are discretionary. The court will try to hear both sides of the case before ordering an injunction unless it is clearly an emergency.

The proceedings

Proceedings take place in the county court for the area in which the premises are located or where the landlord lives.

Complete the claim form N1, available from www.justice.gov.uk/civil/procrules_fin/menus/forms.htm together with a statement of case, listing the cause of action, the relief or remedy sought and the material facts. An application notice should also be completed. Serve the relevant documents on the landlord at least two days before the hearing.

The hearing will be heard by a single judge, possibly in chambers. Often the judge accepts an undertaking from the landlord about future conduct without making a formal order – failing to comply would be contempt of court.

Scotland and Northern Ireland

The laws in Scotland and Northern Ireland differ in places from those in England and Wales. It is these differences that this chapter is concerned with.

Scotland

Housing law in Scotland differs in a variety of ways from the legislation for England and Wales and, on the whole, is more demanding of the landlord. This is only a summary of the major differences ,so always seek independent legal advice.

Unlike England and Wales, where a change of government has led to a halt in activity to increase regulation in the private rental sector, Scotland continues to legislate to improve the sector. This is despite the fact that their own research shows landlords and tenants in Scotland get on very well – according to the Scottish Government, '85 per cent of tenants were either "very or fairly satisfied"'. This research also shows that the majority of landlords are individuals who own one or more properties. Most appear to invest for capital growth as opposed to income.

'There is a gap in landlord and tenant understanding of their legal obligations.'

The research does, however, highlight the fact that there is a gap in landlord and tenant understanding of the rules and regulations they need to abide by. As a result, two very useful websites have been set up to help communicate the information that you need (see below).

Landlord rules, regulations and accreditation

If you are a landlord of a Scottish property or properties (whether you live in Scotland or not), it is important to understand and abide by the rules and regulations, especially since the Private Rented Housing (Scotland) Act 2011 has been introduced.

The Landlord Register

Since April 2006, private landlords of residential properties in Scotland

Websites that explain registration for landlords and tenants in Scotland are **www.scotland.gov.uk/topics/built-environment/housing/privaterent** and **www.landlordregistrationscotland.gov.uk**.

have been required to register with their local authority. To register, you must be able to prove you are a 'fit and proper person' to let a property. Since August 2011, the penalty for not registering is up to £50,000. In addition, the local authority can request a criminal record certificate and charge you up to £1,000 if you don't notify them that you've appointed an agent.

If you are a landlord, you must register with every local authority where you let property (most agents also register). The registration fee is £55 per landlord plus £11 per property registered. If you own a property jointly, such as husband and wife, then you nominate one 'lead owner'. If you are unrelated, both owners need to be registered.

If you are letting out a house in multiple occupancy (HMO), you do not need to register (see right and pages 31–3), as you are covered by your HMO licence.

You can receive a 10 per cent discount on these fees if you apply online and further discounts if you work with multiple authorities. It's essential to know that although an agent can fill in the registration on your behalf, you have to sign it yourself. You are also responsible for notifying any changes and the renewal every three years.

As in the rest of the UK, you must also have an Energy Performance Certificate if you market properties for rent, and abide by the gas, electric, furniture and furnishings safety regulations (see pages 74–8). In addition, any tenancy agreements must be fair, as regulated by the Office of Fair Trading.

With regards to the electrics, you need to ensure they are in a 'reasonable state of repair and proper working order at the start of the tenancy and at all times during the tenancy'. They need to meet the 'tolerable' and 'repairing' standard. To be sure you abide by the law, have the property checked by a competent electrician at the start of each tenancy.

Houses in multiple occupation (HMOs)

Scotland has its own definition of an HMO. The requirements to obtain an HMO licence may differ though from one local authority to another. The Government definition of an HMO is 'A house is an HMO if it is the only or principal residence of three or more qualifying persons from three or more families.' A 'house' is 'any building, or any part of a building occupied as a separate dwelling', so, really, all residential property.

For more on electric regulations, read the pdf 'Landlords' guide to electrical safety' from **www.esc.org.uk** and search for 'Scotland'. The accreditation scheme is on **www.landlordaccreditationscotland.com**. The grounds for possession in Scotland can be seen in full at **www.scotland.gov.uk**.

HMOs typically refer to lets such as student or anyone else that shares a property.

If you let a property as an HMO, you will need to make sure you have a licence or you can be fined up to £50,000. You need to apply to the local authority for an HMO licence. To be accepted, both you and the property are vetted by the local authority and your application is sent to the police and fire authorities. In order to process your application, the property is normally inspected by the local authority and you will have to supply all the relevant safety certificates.

Licence fees vary depending on the local authority and the number of properties. They can be from £400 up to £1,800 initially and can be valid for up to three years when renewal fees are likely to apply.

Private Rented Housing (Scotland) Act

These are the additional rules and regulations that apply to this Act:

- **Include the power to disqualify a landlord** for up to five years.
- **Unregistered agents** can be charged a fee for any checks.
- **All property renting adverts** need to include the Landlord Registration Number (except 'to let' boards).
- **The Private Rented Housing Panel** is required to pass on any details to the local authority that are requested by them.
- **Allow Ministers** to increase the categories for HMO licensing.
- **Give the local authority powers** to address problems of overcrowding in privately rented homes.
- **Landlords and agents** must provide specified information to the tenant at the start of a tenancy.

Landlord (and letting agent) accreditation

In an effort to improve the knowledge of letting rules and regulations, landlords and letting agents can also join a voluntary accreditation scheme. This helps to reassure tenants that you are a good landlord or agent to rent from.

The accreditation scheme is free to individual landlords and for letting agents this varies from £50 to £350 depending on the number of properties managed. To be accredited you need to ensure you meet the Scottish Core Standards for Accredited Landlords and there is an online guide you can download. To find out more and apply, visit www.landlordaccreditationscotland.com.

To find a solicitor in Scotland, look at **www.lawscot.org.uk** and for an HMO guide for landlords, go to **www.scotland.gov.uk**. The Private Rented Housing Panel is at **www.prhpscotland.gov.uk**. For legal housing advice, go to **www.lawscot.org.uk**.

Tenants

It is important for anyone who is renting in Scotland to know that most legal protection only applies to tenancies, which in addition to the requirement for exclusive occupation (as in England) and payment of rent in money or in kind, should set the length of the rental period. If none is agreed, common law may imply a period of one year during which the circumstances of the case allow such an implication to made. At the end of that period, unless the parties have contracted otherwise or any lesser period as the lease provides for under common law, the tenancy automatically renews for the same period unless the landlord or tenant has formally terminated the tenancy at the termination date. This is called 'tacit relocation'.

'The good news for tenants in Scotland is that you only need to ensure your landlord is registered and, ideally, belongs to the Landlord Accreditation Scheme.'

Tenant's take

If you are renting in the private sector, then you have lots of ways to ensure you don't rent from a rogue landlord or rent a property that is unsafe - even more so than in England and Wales. Unfortunately, according to research from the Scottish Government, most tenants don't understand them. For example, 3 per cent of households don't have a tenancy agreement, 7 per cent agreed they don't understand their tenant rights and 2 per cent said they have never had their gas serviced.

The good news for Scottish tenants is that you just need to make sure that your landlord (or letting agent) is registered (see pages 181–2) and, ideally, belongs to the Landlord Accreditation Scheme. Other memberships that landlords or letting agents may belong to include:

- Scottish Association of Landlords
- National Landlords Association
- Scottish Rural Property and Business Association
- National Federation of Residential Landlords

For letting agents they should be members of ARLA and the Property Ombudsman Scheme and/or Royal Institution of Chartered Surveyors, Scotland.

Some rogue landlords might say they are registered and members of organisations. However, this might not be the case so it is important to check their registration online via www.landlordregistrationscotland.gov.uk and with the associations above.

For more help renting a property in Scotland, use our 'Viewing a property' help on page 105 and checklist on page 106 and if you have any problems with your landlord or letting agent during the tenancy, visit www.prhpscotland.gov.uk, who will help with disputes.

The agreement must be in writing if the tenancy is to last for more than a year. Licences are rarely used in Scotland: the courts have a wide definition of 'tenancy' and what is accepted as a licence in England might be classified as a tenancy north of the border. Licensees have fewer rights than tenants, especially regarding security of tenure.

Private-sector tenancies

Tenants in the private sector are still small – accounting for approximately 7 per cent of housing stock – and they have different rights to those in the public sector.

Assured tenancies

These were introduced to revitalise the Scottish private rented sector from 2 January 1989. An assured tenancy is essentially a tenancy at a market rent with a reduced degree of security. Assured tenancy agreements must be in writing and the tenant must be given a copy free of charge. If the tenancy has been terminated by a notice to quit or if it was inherited, the landlord can still increase the rent provided there is provision to do so in the tenancy agreement in the form of a formula or a specified rise. If there is no such provision, the rent can only be raised by a more complicated procedure and the tenant has the right to go to the Private Rented Housing Panel.

'Assured tenancy agreements must be in writing and the tenant must be given a copy free of charge.'

- **Succession:** An assured tenancy can be inherited by a spouse provided the house was his only or principal home at the time of death. The tenancy is called a statutory assured tenancy and can only be inherited once.
- **Security of tenure:** The general principal of security of tenure applies, so even after the contractual tenancy has been ended (for example, by a notice to quit), the tenant can stay under a statutory assured tenancy until the landlord recovers possession through a court order.
- **Obtaining possession:** To obtain an order for recovery of possession the landlord must do the following things
  - Serve notice on the tenant, specifying the grounds.
  - Terminate the contractual assured tenancy at its 'ish' (termination date or lease expiry) with notice to quit of at least 28 days.

- Raise an 'action for recovery for possession of heritable property' in the sheriff court for the area where the house is located. If the sheriff accepts one of grounds 1-8 of schedule 5 to the Housing (Scotland) Act 1988 are established, he must grant decree. If only one of grounds 9-17 are established, he may grant decree. The decree is issued two weeks later. The grounds for recovery are similar to those under English legislation (see pages 168–9).

Short assured tenancies

Introduced by the Housing (Scotland) Act 1988, these give little security of tenure. They are created when the landlord gives, prior to the creation of the tenancy, the proposed tenant a formal notice (the AT5) stating it will be a short assured tenancy. The term must be for a fixed period of not less than six months, which automatically renews unless either party gives formal notice otherwise. Although after the initial six-month period ends, the tenancy tends to roll on a month-on-month basis. A form of wording in the tenancy is required to cover this practice to ensure 'tacit relocation' doesn't happen.

In the past, a tenant could go to the Rent Assessment Committee (RAC) if the rent was thought to be too high. However, the RAC was absorbed into the Private Rented Housing Panel in September 2007 and now a rent can only be lowered if it is set significantly higher than the market rate.

- **Recovering possession:** No reason need be given when requesting an order for possession, and the sheriff must grant it if:
  - The tenancy has reached termination.
  - A valid Notice to Quit is served timeously (that is, in time which would be 40 clear days before the ish) and competently (in accordance with legislative requirements) preventing tacit relocation and terminating the tenancy at its ish.
  - No further contractual tenancy is in existence.
  - At least two months' notice has been given, followed by an AT6 (if the owner is repossessing) and a Section 33 notice.

Better repairs

To make sure landlords can make repairs, they are allowed to access the property in the case of an emergency and at a 'reasonable time' if 24 hours notice has been given. If they do not comply with repairing obligations, tenants can report them to the PRHP.

Protected tenancies

Very few of these tenancies remain as none have been created since 1989. For advice on a protected tenancy, consult a solicitor with experience in this area.

Statutory tenancies

A statutory tenancy offers similar rights to a protected or Assured or Short Assured tenancy and arises when a tenant remains in possession of a house after the contractual tenancy has been terminated (that is, by a notice to quit) or a tenant succeeded to the tenancy before 1990.

No repair, no rent

On 3 September 2007, the Repairing Standard in Terms of the Housing (Scotland) Act 2006 was introduced. The purpose of the Act is to ensure that private landlords keep a let home suitable for 'human habitation' and to bring into line the regulations in the private rental sector so they are similar to those in the social sector.

Work on the property must be carried out to meet the repairing standards set out in this Act. The landlord is responsible for keeping the property and fixtures and fittings in a reasonable state of repair and in proper working order, for example:

- Making the property wind and watertight.
- The structure and exterior, including drains, gutters and pipes.
- Water and gas piping and electric wiring.
- Basins, sinks, baths and toilets.
- Any fixtures and fittings, such as gas fires and water heaters.
- The house needs to have satisfactory provision for detecting fires and for giving warning in the event of a fire or suspected fire.

If the landlord does not do this, sometimes the tenant withholds (but does not spend) rent equivalent to the amount owed for the service or problem. However, if a tenant, you must follow the procedure set out in your contract to the letter, or you risk the landlord taking action against you for non-payment of rent. If you are considering this, do not do so until you have obtained guidance from Citizens Advice, Shelter or a solicitor.

Assigning and subletting

Assured tenants cannot assign, sublet or part with possession of any part of the property without the landlord's consent – and this can be refused without giving reasons. A permitted sub-tenant becomes a tenant of the landlord if the other tenancy ends for any reason.

'Common law tenants can stop other people entering without permission.'

Harassment and eviction

Provision to prevent harassment and illegal eviction is similar to that of English law although it is always essential to seek specialist legal advice.

Common law tenancies

If your tenancy is not regulated by any other laws, you still have rights under common law, which may apply if:

- **The landlord is also resident** in the house, using the property as their only or main home. A separate flat in the property does not meet this definition, and the landlord needn't own the house – he could be a tenant who is subletting.
- **The tenant is a student** in university-owned accommodation.
- **The landlord is in the police** or fire service.
- **The tenant is homeless,** living in temporary accommodation provided by the council.

Common law tenants have the right to possession, meaning they should be able to stop other people entering without permission.

- **Other people can only move** in to share the property with the consent of the landlord.
- **The agreement will automatically repeat** ('tacit relocation') unless either party gives notice otherwise.
- **Either party can give notice to quit** in writing at any time (although such notice may only apply at the termination date), giving four weeks' notice on a six-month let or 40 days on a year's lease. However, if the tenancy is not due to expire, the landlord can only ask the tenant to leave if they have broken a condition of the tenancy agreement and under specific grounds, getting an order from a sheriff.

Public-sector tenancies

Most public-sector tenancies granted since 30 September 2002 are Scottish secure tenancies. These were created in the Housing (Scotland) Act 2001 and mean that virtually all tenants of local authorities and registered social landlords have the same terms of a single, common tenancy. Prior to this, council tenancies were termed 'secure tenancies', governed by the Housing (Scotland) Act 1987, while most housing association tenancies were assured tenancies governed by the Housing (Scotland) Act 1988. Exceptions to this change are:

- Short assured tenants' of registered social landlords remain short assured tenants.
- Some tenants will be given 'short Scottish secure tenancies' instead of 'Scottish secure tenancies'.

Scottish secure tenancies (SSTs) and short SSTs are complicated and if you have any issues, it is important to consult a legal specialist for your specific circumstances.

Northern Ireland

To make sure landlords can make repairs, they are allowed to access the property in the case of an emergency and at a 'reasonable time' if 24 hours notice has been given.

The private sector

In June 2011, new legislation was introduced that makes changes to the way the private rental sector operates. This, together with changes made in 2007 (and still more planned for 2013) together with investor landlords buying and letting new, high-quality properties, means the private rental sector has improved in Northern Ireland from a tenant's perspective.

In the past, there were two types of tenancy agreement: controlled or uncontrolled. The main changes affect the controlled tenancy agreements, but also impact on the uncontrolled tenancies, because if they don't pass a fitness inspection, they will become 'interim controlled' until they do.

Controlled tenancy

A tenancy that is controlled is one that hasn't passed a fitness inspection report (see box, opposite) and used to include restricted and regulated tenancies and protected shorthold tenancies.

- **Restricted tenancies and regulated tenancies.** Restricted tenancies are usually old, small terraced houses in poor repair. The rent was set at its 1978 level of around £1 per week. A landlord can modernise the property and apply for it to become a regulated tenancy. Under a controlled tenancy, restricted and regulated tenancies essentially stay the same, but tenants who have succession rights (see page 143) will now only be allowed one succession right.
- **Protected shorthold tenancies** have been abolished and become uncontrolled tenancies.

If a landlord wishes to increase the rent on a restricted or regulated

For more information on the possible introduction of a tenancy deposit scheme, visit **www.dsdni.gov.uk/index/hsdiv-housing/private_rented_sector.htm** and look out for free landlord seminars provided by your local authority.

The fitness inspection report

Once a tenancy is ready for renewal, or a landlord wishes to increase the rent, a fitness inspection report is carried out. This is a report made by the local district council, which assesses the fitness of a property for someone to live in. It is normally made at the request of the landlord but sometimes it can be at the request of a tenant if the property has fallen into disrepair.

The inspection costs £50 and, should it be passed, the landlord is then free to charge any rent.

However, if the fitness inspection report highlights any repairs that are required, the rent will then be controlled by the rent officer for Northern Ireland until the work has been done and a second - successful - inspection (costing £100) is made. This will check and assess factors that affect the property's condition such as:

- Structural stability.
- Any levels of damp (which could cause health problems).
- Provision for heating, lighting and ventilation.
- Adequate supply of water.
- Bathroom and waste water facilities.
- Kitchen and cooking facilities.

tenancy agreement, he or she has to apply to the rent officer and must have passed a fitness inspection report unless the property meets any of the following criteria:

- **Was built post 1945**; or
- **Had a regulated rent certificate** in the last ten years.
- **Was given a renovation grant** by the Housing Executive in the last ten years.
- **Was granted an HMO** within the last ten years.

If the fitness inspection report has not been carried out, the rent officer will set the rent on the assumption that the property does not meet the standards. If the property has been inspected by the district council, they forward the information to the rent officer.

Uncontrolled tenancy

Tenants in uncontrolled properties have increased rights. Before the new legislation, they would be entitled to a rent book, freedom from harassment and illegal eviction, a notice to quit period of 28 days, due process of law and the

For more details of the changes in legislation, visit **www.nidirect.gov.uk/what-is-rent-control**. For information about HMOs (see pages 30-1) in Northern Ireland, go to **www.housingadviceni.org/migrant-workers-sharing-accommodation.html**.

Licensed to pay bills

Licensees have fewer rights than tenants. A license applies if:

- The landlord is resident in the property.
- The accommodation is a student hall of residence or a hostel.
- The occupant is sharing with friends or family.

right to claim Housing Benefit. Now, the tenant must also be given a copy of the tenancy agreement, or at least a statement in writing of the terms of their tenancy.

Public-sector tenancies

Social housing is regulated by the Northern Ireland Housing Executive (NIHE), and application forms for accommodation can be downloaded from its website. Tenants' rights are similar to those offered in social housing in England and Wales.

The NIHE operates a rent scheme to calculate the rent on most of its properties, based on points given according to fitness, age, design and amenities. A rent calculator (see below) allows tenants to estimate the rent payable on the type of house they need, and to see if their current rent is correct.

Useful contacts

Northern Ireland Housing Executive (NIHE): www.nihe.gov.uk
Citizens Advice: www.citizensadvice.co.uk
sing Rights Service: www. housingrights.org.uk
Northern Ireland Ombudsman: www.ni-ombudsman.org.uk (deals with complaints against social housing).

For more information about uncontrolled tenancies, go to **www.nihe.gov.uk/renting_privately_a_strategic_framework.pdf**. To calculate the rent due on NIHE housing, go to **www.nihe.gov.uk**.

Checking your agreement

12

Most of the time people rent and let out property without any problems. It's only when they do occur that we realise how important contractual agreements are. Rather than wait until then, whether you are a landlord or a tenant, make sure you get an independent legal lettings expert to check the contract and recommend changes.

Assured shorthold agreements

Most private tenancies between a landlord and tenant are assured shorthold tenancies (ASTs) and their main points are explained in this section.

This agreement lasts for up to six months (but could have a fixed term of many years) after which the landlord can claim possession through a court order, should the need arise. However, there is some protection for tenants against excessive rent.

The clauses highlighted on pages 191–9 are the main ones that you will see in an agreement. Although they run consecutively throughout this chapter, they may appear in a different order in the agreement you see.

The sample clauses covered in this section relate only to assured shorthold tenancies, so are not necessarily relevant to a company let.

BE CAREFUL!

All guidance notes and clauses in this chapter are examples only and need to be used in conjunction with chapters 7 and 8. All explanations and notes are given throughout in square brackets.

Help is at hand!

The National Landlords Association (NLA) have introduced a facility for members as well as non-members to access up-to-date legal documents for free, including a range of tenancy agreements, forms and letters to help landlords manage most tenancies.

You can create these documents online, then print or print and fill in by hand. Visit www.landlords.org.uk for more information. If you are not sure whether to sign an agreement as a tenant or landlord, then visit your local Citizens Advice Bureau, contact Shelter or seek advice from a legal lettings expert.

To see a letting agreement checklist, go to **www.which.co.uk/renting-checklist.** Visit **www.landlords.org.uk** for help with increasing rent, property inspections and ending a tenancy.

Top 10 dos and don'ts for ASTs

1 Don't sign a tenancy agreement unless it is easy to read and you have read every clause. If in any doubt, get it checked out by a legal expert.

2 Do ensure you take time (two days or more is acceptable) to check the agreement.

3 Don't sign an agreement that clearly includes clauses that don't apply, such as an agreement given to you by a landlord that is renting to you privately, but frequently mentions or refers to 'letting agent', or keeping a garden tidy when there isn't one!

4 Make sure that you have read and understood every clause in the tenancy agreement - if in doubt, ask an independent party BEFORE you sign.

5 Check that along with the agreement you have information about the tenancy deposit protection scheme (see pages 83-4).

6 As a tenant or landlord, query any clauses that are too 'onerous', such as 'no pets allowed' (see page 142).

7 If you are a landlord accepting a guarantor, make sure that the guarantor is present during the signing of the agreement to ensure they agree and understand the responsibility they are taking on. If this isn't possible, make sure you speak to them and they fully understand what they are signing.

8 Get a legal lettings specialist to check any additions or alterations to an agreement (otherwise changes you make could invalidate the agreement).

9 If you are a landlord, make sure you have met all the tenants that will be renting your property and check they have all signed the agreement.

10 Do ensure any new letting agreements are up to date with the latest legal changes.

Definitions

Some legal agreements are very confusing as they use a lot of legal terminology as opposed to 'plain English'. Here are the most used legal terms in a lettings contract:

- **'Agreement':** meaning, the tenancy agreement you sign. It usually states 'including any variation or amendment of it', which allows for specific changes to be made that could be requested by the tenant or the landlord or to adapt to changes in the law.
- **'Contents':** the landlord's fixtures, fittings, furniture and contents that belong to the landlord, listed in an attached inventory.
- **'Deposit':** the amount that a tenant normally pays to cover the landlord for rent arrears and if the tenant fails to fulfil his or her obligations.

- **'Term':** the amount of time agreed for the tenancy (normally a fixed term of six months for an AST agreement). Some agents insist on a 12-month agreement, which ties you into this term, and then offers one to two months' notice (for both the landlord and tenant) to end the agreement. However, watch out – some agreements may not give you this six-month break clause, and it is vital to make sure you have an agreement checked with an independent legal lettings expert.

Some agreements may also give a summary of the 'key parts of the agreements' or these may be included in other clauses.

- **'the Term':** '...... months from and including ...... [specify commencement date], including any extension or holding over whether under the Housing Act 1988 or otherwise'.
- **'the Property':** [insert full postal address of property to be let].
- **'the Deposit':** '£..... pounds' [stating the amount in figures].
- **'the Rent':** '£........ pounds each month/week, payable in advance on the ... day of each month/week, the first payment payable .... and the method of payment [for example, direct debit].
- **'the Interest Rate':** '4 per cent [ranges from 4 to 6 per cent] per year above the base lending rate of .... Bank plc [should state the name of the bank]'.

Particulars of parties involved

This typically refers to contact details of all those involved in the let. It may include reference to a 'guarantor' or 'relevant party', should a third party be supporting the tenant (see pages 200–01).

Date of contract

This is typically the day that the contract becomes binding and is therefore likely to be the start of the tenancy.

Parties involved in the agreement

As a landlord, try to ensure the address given by the tenant isn't just the property he or she is currently letting, but also an address where you can contact the tenant after the tenancy has ended.

As a tenant, ask for it to be clear how and who you contact if there is an emergency.

To aid communication, it is also advisable to have other ways to contact the parties concerned, such as an email and telephone number (preferably a landline and mobile).

'The date of the contract will be the start of the tenancy.'

Clause examples: parties involved in the agreement

Parties
The Landlord: ....whose address is ....
[insert landlord's name, full postal address and contact telephone/email]

The Tenant: ....whose address is ....
[insert tenant's name, address and contact telephone/email]

The Letting Agent .... whose address is ....
[insert letting agent's name, office address and contact telephone/email]

'Make sure there's a data protection clause to protect yourself.'

Data protection

An additional clause that should be included is to cover circumstances where the landlord/agent can share the tenant's details with required third parties, such as the inventory clerk or utility companies, should there be any problems after the tenancy.

The property

These clauses usually define what constitutes 'The Property' and should include the property's address and the terms:

- **'fixtures and fittings':** for example, light fittings, fireplace, kitchen and bathroom fittings.
- **'effects set out in the inventory':** for example, a phone, washing machine, cleaning bucket.
- **'outside space' or 'garden':** for example, a garden, driveway, walls or fencing owned by the landlord.

The deposit

This is one of the most important clauses to look for in an agreement – especially if you are the tenant. It is covered in more detail earlier in the book (see pages 83–4). The types of clauses that will apply may include those shown in the box on page 194.

Clauses relating to interest on the deposit

One of the questions often asked is who keeps the interest from the deposit monies held? Tenants often think it should be paid to them, but this may not be the case if the agreement says otherwise. Indeed, The DPS (see page 83) scheme is free because part of its costs are

Clause examples: the deposit

1. The Landlord holds the deposit as security for:
   a. unpaid Rent or other money lawfully due to the Landlord; and unpaid accounts for gas, electricity, telephone, television licence, Council Tax, water and environmental and sewage charges;
   b. any other breach of the Tenant's Obligations; and
   c. any other claims made against the Landlord because of any acts or omissions of the Tenant.
2. The Landlord may, where it is reasonable to do so, take money from the Deposit:
   a. to cover the matters listed in Clause 1 above; and
   b. to pay on the Tenant's behalf the charges mentioned in the rest of the agreement; and
   c. to pay for gas, electricity, telephone and water services to be reconnected, if disconnected due to the Tenant's default.

The return of the tenant's deposit

1. Subject to clauses [which would result in the landlord keeping all or part of the deposit] set out in the Tenancy Deposit Protection Scheme rules, if the Tenant:
   a. complies with the Tenant's Obligations; and
   b. vacates the Property; and
   c. returns all the Property keys; and
   d. both the tenant and the landlord agree on any deductions then the Deposit (or the balance of it, if any), without interest, will be refunded to the Tenant, or where the Tenant is more than one person, to any of them, within 10 days of the Tenant and Landlord/Letting agent agreeing on the amount to be repaid.
2. If the amount lawfully due at the end of tenancy is more than the amount of the Deposit, the Tenant must reimburse the Landlord/Agent the excess within 14 days of the money being requested.

paid for by the interest generated from the deposit with the rest being refunded to either the tenant or landlord. In other cases it may be the landlord or the letting agent that keeps the interest. For example:

'the Deposit (or the balance of it, if any) will be repaid without interest to the tenant', OR it may state who keeps the interest, for example: ' the Landlord or the Letting Agent'.

A further clause that may be added explains what happens if the landlord sells the property on, with the tenant still within the property (see the clause example, top box on page 195).

'Tenancy deposit protection schemes have streamlined who holds what money and where.'

Clause examples: the deposit if the property is sold

If the Landlord: sells his interest in the Property; and pays the Deposit (or balance of it, if any) to his buyer, the Tenant shall release the previous owner from all claims and liabilities in respect of the Deposit.

Rent clauses

These clauses cover everything that is relevant to paying rent, including how much, payment method, rental increases and what happens if the rent isn't paid (see the clause examples box below). In some agreements, these clauses may come under the tenant and landlord obligations (see pages 197–9) or in the summary information at the start.

There are two ways of dealing with rent in an agreement:

- Rent information can be mentioned specifically in the AST (as below) OR
- The agreement may refer to a 'Section 13 notice', which advises that a tenant's rent is going to be increased (see page 145).

'Rent clauses tell you how much to pay, when, increases and what happens if it's not paid.'

Clause examples: the rent

1. 'the Rent': £... (.......pounds) each month/week, payable in advance on the ... day of each month/week, the first payment payable .... and the method of payment [for example, direct debit].
2. To pay to the Landlord/Agent the Rent by [direct debit or other payment method] into the Landlord's/Agent's Bank Account according to the terms of the Agreement.
3. To pay to the Landlord on demand:
   a. interest at the following Interest Rate (......) on the Rent if the Rent or other money is not paid on time; and
   b. sufficient money to make up the deposit to its original amount; and
4. Unless a court orders otherwise, the tenant will pay Landlord's reasonable legal costs and expenses (including VAT), properly incurred, in:
   a. recovering Rent or other money from the Tenant; and
   b. enforcing the Agreement; and
   c. serving any notice on the Tenant in connection with the enforcement of the Tenant's Obligations; and
   d. recovering possession from the Tenant.

Clause examples: rent increases

1. The Landlord may increase the rent by giving Tenant .... months' notice in writing prior to a rent payment day specifying the amount of the new rent.
2. The Tenant will then pay the increased amount as the Rent on and from that rent payment day.
3. If the Tenant does not agree to the amount specified, he may give the Landlord not less than one month's notice in writing, expiring on any day [if the tenancy is periodic, then the notice should expire at the end of the period of the tenancy], terminating the tenancy from that day.

Rent increases are allowed for ASTs. However, courts have ruled that rent increase clauses die when the tenancy becomes statutory periodic. A Section 13 notice of the Housing Act 1988 must be used for a statutory periodic. Rent increases are sensitive to introduce to tenants so it is essential either to have the clauses on rental agreements clearly in the tenancy agreement or seek specialist lettings legal advice if you apply to increase the rent under Section 13 of the Housing Act 1988.

Possession and notices

These clauses explain how you need to give notice that as a tenant

Clause examples: notices

1. Under section 48 of the Landlord and Tenant Act 1987 notices by the Tenant are to be left at, sent via ordinary post or sent by recorded delivery post to, the Landlord's/Agent's address as set out as below.
2. In the case of notices to be served on the Tenant, unless the Tenant has notified the Landlord of another address, they will be sent to the Property or the last known address of the Tenant.
3. If anyone is lawfully residing at the Property or if the tenancy is an assured shorthold tenancy, the Landlord must obtain a court order for possession of the Property before re-entering it.
4. If at any time the Landlord:
   a. requires the Property for occupation by himself or any member of his family; or
   b. wishes to sell the Property with vacant possession; or
   c. has died and the Landlord's personal representatives require vacant possession either to sell the Property or so that it can be occupied by a beneficiary under the Landlord's will or intestacy then.

   In any such case, the Landlord may terminate the tenancy by serving not less than two months' notice in writing.

you want to quit the tenancy or as a landlord, take the property back into your possession. It is a complex area and, as such, is described in detail on pages 160–71.

Tenant's obligations

Whether you are a tenant or a landlord, it is really important to read these clauses carefully so you understand what is expected. Clauses that explain the tenant's obligations are extensive. They can appear in a list or in a series of separate clauses (as on pages 198–9).

Landlord's obligations

Some agreements don't have a separate section covering a landlord's obligations, as they are defined by law, so you may find that the clauses listed in the box below are specifically referred to in the agreement under headings such as 'Quiet Enjoyment'; 'Notices' or 'Insurance'.

As with tenant's obligations, it is imperative that both landlord and tenant understand these obligations. If you are a landlord and outsource the let to a letting agent, then it is crucial that you are clear – and have in writing (see pages 200–4) – which parts of the letting agreement you are responsible for and which the letting agent is responsible for.

Fair wear and tear

The fair wear and tear clause is often an area for confusion, and it

Clause examples: landlord's obligations

1. Quiet enjoyment
   The Landlord may keep keys to the Property, but during the Term may only enter the Property at reasonable times and on reasonable written notice [being at least 24 hours] having been given [except in cases of emergency].
2. Insurance
   The Landlord will supply a copy of the insurance policy and must purchase suitable insurance cover for the property which covers the property's fixtures and fittings; anything owned by the Landlord such as appliances and standard risks such as loss or damage from flooding, fire, storms, burst pipes. The Tenant must insure their own belongings under a separate insurance policy and can have the option to insure the Landlord's items against accidental damage caused by themselves.
3. Repair and Maintenance
   Under the Landlord & Tenant Act 1985 (as amended) the Landlord must keep good repair the structure and exterior of the Property and keep in repair and proper working order the installations in the Property for the supply of water, gas, electricity, sanitation and for space and water heating.

Clause examples: tenant's obligations

1. Replacing locks and keys if the Tenant loses any keys or breaches other security clauses; and
2. To pay during the Term a proportionate part of:
   a. the Council Tax for the Property; and
   b. the water, sewerage and environmental charges for the Property; and
   c. the television licence fee for the Property.
3. Keep the Property and Contents clean and in good decorative repair, and in particular to:
   a. remove rubbish from the Property regularly; and
   b. protect the Property from frost damage; and
   c. ensure rooms are properly ventilated; and
   d. clean the inside of all windows regularly; and
   e. vacuum-clean all carpets regularly; and
   f. not to block any drains, pipes, sinks, basins or baths; and
   g. keep the garden tidy; and
   h. cut the grass regularly during the growing season; and
   i. not to allow the Property to become infested with vermin of any kind.
4. To comply with notices from the Landlord to remedy breaches of other clauses within a reasonable time. Not to, or allow anyone else to:
   a. Do anything that would cause the Landlord's insurance policy to become ineffective; or
   b. damage the Property or Contents; or
   c. remove the Contents from the Property; or
   d. change the locks at the Property; or
   e. alter, add or attach anything to the Property; or
   f. tamper with the water, telephone, gas or electricity systems and installations serving the Property; or
   g. overload, block up or damage any drains, pipes, wires or cables serving the Property; or
   h. assault or abuse the Landlord, the Landlord's agents or any members of the Landlord's family.
5. To notify the Landlord promptly of:
   a. any vermin, defects or disrepair in the Property or Contents; and
   b. any notices or mail addressed to the Landlord delivered to the Property.
6. To permit the Landlord and/or his Agent(s) to enter the Property at all reasonable times and on reasonable written notice [being at least 24 hours] having been given [except in cases of emergency] to:
   a. inspect the Property and Contents; or
   b. repair the Property; or
   c. repair or replace any of the Contents; or
   d. replace the locks at the Property; or
   e. comply with any legal obligations; or
   f. show prospective buyers or tenants around the Property.

7. Not to do or allow at the Property anything which:
   a. might cause a nuisance or annoyance to others; or
   b. is dangerous; or
   c. is illegal or immoral.
8. Not to, or allow others to keep any birds and animals at the Property (other than in secure cages or containers) without the consent of the Landlord, such consent not to be unreasonably withheld or delayed.
9. To ensure that all windows and doors are properly secured when the property is unattended.
10. Not to:
    a. assign; or
    b. underlet; or
    c. part with; or
    d. share possession of the Property or any part of it without the Landlord's consent, such consent not to be unreasonably withheld or delayed.
11. On the termination of the tenancy to return to the Landlord:
    a. the Property and the Contents in a clean and tidy condition in accordance with the Tenant's Obligations; and
    b. all keys to the Property.

is important for both the landlord and the tenant to understand what is considered to be fair wear and tear, and what is 'damage' to the property. Typical wording for this clause would be:

'The Tenant is not liable for fair wear and tear to the Property or Contents and is not liable to put the Property or Contents into a better condition than they were in at the commencement date of the Term.'

An example of fair wear and tear would be a carpet that becomes threadbare as opposed to a carpet that has been damaged in a way that wouldn't be classed as 'reasonable', such as holes caused by cigarettes. An inventory is essential to help with this issue.

To help avoid disputes over fair wear and tear versus damage, a qualified inventory clerk should be employed (see page 86).

Signing the agreement

Finally, once you are happy with all the clauses in the agreement, the relevant parties will need to sign it. The witnesses should ideally be someone independent of the landlord and tenant – so not necessarily a relative.

Other clauses

Agreements vary dramatically so you may find clauses other than the ones highlighted here. Some of these clauses are specific to certain circumstances, such as when a third party (for example, a parent) pays the deposit.

Other forms of agreement

There are two other forms of agreement that are used regularly: a guarantee agreement, where someone other than the tenant acts as a guarantor should the tenant default, and a terms of business letter, between a landlord and letting agent.

Guarantee agreement

The guarantee agreement is where someone (other than the tenant) agrees to 'insure' the landlord for the tenant's deposit value. The relevant clauses for the guarantor can either be added into the AST agreement or offered as a separate agreement with the particulars of parties involved (with the addition of the guarantor's details) and the property information at the start of the agreement and the signing details at the end.

The guarantor

A guarantor agrees to pay the rent should the tenant default. It is usually a parent who signs the agreement, but it could be anyone or more than one person (for example, mother and father) if required. The guarantor can also agree to pay the deposit on the tenant's behalf. There is no legal requirement for who can be a guarantor, but ensure that they know what they have signed, are happy to be a guarantor and, most especially, have the money available!

Terms of business agreement

This is an agreement that a landlord has to sign when handing over the full or part responsibility for letting a property to a letting agent. The most important details in a terms of business agreement are outlined on pages 202–4.

'Always read a terms of business agreement before signing it.'

BE CAREFUL!

Many landlords sign a terms of business agreement without even reading through it. It can be anything from a few pages to more than fifty, but however long it is, it is essential that as a landlord when you are considering an agent, this is one of the first things you read. Don't leave it until you have chosen your agent.

Clause examples: the guarantor

It is agreed as follows:

1. In consideration of the Landlord granting the Tenant a tenancy of the Property upon the terms of the Agreement, the Guarantor guarantees:
   a. the payment by the Tenant of the rent and any other monies lawfully due to the Landlord under the Agreement; and
   b. the performance and observance by the Tenant of all the other terms contained or implied in the Agreement.
2. The Guarantor covenants with the Landlord as follows:
   a. If the Tenant defaults in the payment of the rent or any other monies lawfully due to the Landlord under the Agreement, the Guarantor will promptly upon written demand by the Landlord pay to the Landlord the full amount owing from the Tenant.
   b. If the Tenant defaults in the performance or observance of any of the terms contained or implied in the Agreement, the Guarantor will promptly upon written demand by the Landlord pay to the Landlord all reasonable losses, damages, expenses and costs which the Landlord has reasonably incurred because of the Tenant's breaches.
3. It is agreed that this Guarantee cannot be revoked by the Guarantor:
   a. for so long as the tenancy created by the Agreement continues;
4. This Guarantee is not to be revoked by:
   a. the death of the Guarantor [or any of the Guarantors]; or
   b. the death of the Tenant [or any of the Tenants]; or
   c. the bankruptcy of the Tenant [or any of the Tenants].
5. This Guarantee continues in operation:
   a. notwithstanding any alteration of the terms of the Agreement including any increase in the amount of the rent payable for the Property; and
   b. in relation to any new or further tenancy entered into between the Tenant and the Landlord; and
   c. in relation to any statutory periodic tenancy which may arise in the Tenant's favour under the Housing Act 1988; and
   d. notwithstanding that the Agreement may be terminated during the term by agreement, court order, notice, re-entry, forfeiture or otherwise; and
   e. notwithstanding any arrangement made between the Landlord and the Tenant (whether or not with the Guarantor's consent) nor by any indulgence or forbearance shown by the Landlord to the Tenant.
6. This Guarantee constitutes the Guarantor as principal debtor.
7. Any demand by the Landlord under the terms of this Guarantee shall be validly made if sent by registered or recorded delivery post or left at the address(es) specified above as the Guarantor's address or such other address(es) as the Guarantor may notify to the Landlord.
8. Where there is more than one Guarantor, the Guarantor's Obligations will be joint and individual.
9. Where there is more than one Tenant, references in this Guarantee to 'the Tenant' shall be construed as referring to all or both or either or any of the persons so named.

Services on offer

These are likely to include:

- Tenant find, which is where the landlord only pays the agent to find a tenant and thereafter the landlord is responsible for the let while the tenant is in the property.
- Let only.
- Let with rent collection.
- Full management.

Pre-instruction

These clauses include information such as:

- **The landlord appoints the agent** to act on their behalf.
- **The landlord must comply** with the following regulations:
  - Gas Safety (Installation and Use) Regulations 1998.
  - Plugs and Sockets Etc (Safety) Regulations 1994 and Electrical Equipment (Safety) Regulations 1994.
  - Furniture and Furnishings (Fire) (Safety) Regulations 1988.
  - Usually a minimum of one smoke alarm per floor (although this is not a legal requirement, it is a good idea to do this as a landlord).
  - Building regulations.
- **The landlord must give the following information** and confirmation:
  - That the property is clean and fit to rent out.
  - If a leasehold property, that the landlord has permission to rent out the property.
  - If the property is mortgaged, that the landlord has permission from the lender to rent out the property.
  - If the agent doesn't handle the deposit, it is the landlord's responsibility to protect it via one of the deposit protection schemes (see page 83).
- **The landlord must confirm there is adequate insurance cover** for the property or purchase it from the letting agent. Most agents will charge a 10 per cent fee (excluding VAT) for handling insurance claims. If an agent is either directly selling or offering to handle claims insurance for you, they MUST be registered with the Financial Services Authority (FSA) and must be on their letterhead. To find a registered IFA, go to www.fsa.gov.uk.

Fees

These can vary dramatically and make the difference between what is a competitive full management fee and one where you are being stung with charges you thought were included. It is important, therefore, that at the outset you establish if the agent:

- **Is entitled to commission** earned as set out in the scale of charges.
- **Will make any additional charges** (this may be set out in the scale of charges only).
- **Is required to give notice to the landlord** for increasing their charges (usually two months).

- **Can keep the interest earned** on the rental income from their account to when it is deposited in the landlord's account and, in some cases, that they can all keep interest on deposits that are held.
- **Can claim back any costs incurred** due to errors made by the landlord or the agent spending money to comply with the letting's contract.
- **Can impose additional charges** for looking after any insurance claims.
- **Can charge for statements given to third parties,** such as accountants.
- **Is duty bound to release information** on monies the landlord earns to the HMRC if requested.

If letting property to a tenant on Housing Benefit, there will also be a clause that ensures any money collected in rent by the agent classed as an overpayment will have to be reimbursed to the local authority. The landlord will then have to pay back the agent the monies previously received.

Scale of charges

A good agent will give a landlord one sheet of paper explaining all the charges the landlord will incur during the tenancy. It should also outline any 'additional' work and how much it will cost on an hourly rate so you know in advance how much you would pay before you sign up with the agent. The scale of charges should include the following items.

- **An amount that the letting agent** may hold back for emergencies in your account, for example £250.
- **What is and isn't included** in each of the services provided, such as:
  - Visits to the property are sometimes included in full management charges, other times they are additional.
  - Set-up fees may include the cost of an inventory (for checking in and out), or they may charge extra.
  - Tenancy agreements may be included in letting the property or they may be charged extra.
  - Notification of whether the agent charges a percentage fee for organising tradesmen into the landlord's property.

Normally agents will charge for repairs are follows:

- No additional fee; or
- 10 per cent over a fixed cost of works, for example £250 or £500; or
- 10 per cent on all works organised by the agent.

Typical costs to be aware of include the following:

- **Costs of different services:**
  - Tenant Find.
  - Let only.
  - Let with rent collection.
  - Full management. Some agents charge a lower full management fee the more

years that you let the property through them, so check whether the charges are the same ongoing or if you can negotiate lower fees after the first year.

- **There may be clauses that charge other fees,** such as:
  - Professional hourly rate for additional work.
  - Property visits to empty properties.
  - Re-signing fee for the tenant.
  - Costs of inventory, energy performance certificates (see page 54), gas and electrical safety certificates.
- **Whether the costs quoted include VAT or not,** which is 20 per cent, so for every £100 costs incurred, this is actually £20. By law, the OFT require all consumer contracts to include VAT.
- **Handling deposit disputes,** such as preparation work for dispute resolution.
- **Some agents may charge you banking transfer fees** – these can add up, so check whether this is free or not when comparing the cost of different letting agents.

Exclusion of liability or indemnity clause

This is a clause that protects the agent from any claims that may be made against them that are due to the landlord's errors.

Termination of agreement

This can vary dramatically from one agent to another but typically will state that you have to give one to two months' notice to the agent that you wish to end your arrangement. If you pull out of the letting agreement once a tenant has been found but not yet moved in, there may be a charge that you have to pay for pulling out at this late stage.

BE CAREFUL!

Do not sign a terms of business agreement that states 'other charges are available on request' without getting a full list of charges and checking the agreement with an independent legal lettings expert.

Glossary

Accelerated possession procedure (APP): A way for landlords to gain possession of their property quickly and cheaply, without a court hearing.

Accreditation scheme: A voluntary system for checking that landlords offer a reasonable service, which are often run by local authorities or other interested parties.

Assured shorthold tenancy (AST): Now the most common form of tenancy, at the end of which the landlord can repossess the property.

Assured tenancy: A type of tenancy which offers the tenant good security of tenure.

Buy to let: Buying a property in order to let it to a paying tenant.

Buying off plan: Purchasing un-built property from the plans.

County court judgement (CCJ): A judgement for debt recorded at a county court, which will show up in a credit check.

Credit check: Check on a person's credit rating which will show if they pay their bills. Usually carried out by a credit reference agency.

Deposit: A sum of money that is paid in advance to cover any potential costs of damage to the rented property or should you fail to pay the rent. If there is no damage when you leave the property, all the deposit should be returned to you.

DSS: Department for Social Security, now part of the Department of Work and Pensions. DSS is still used as a term describing tenants who receive Housing Benefit.

Energy Performance Certificate (EPC): This rates your home on how much energy it takes to keep it warm and lit. It gives information on how much it costs and what you can do to make your home more energy efficient and reduce carbon dioxide emissions.

Eviction: Forced, legal removal of a tenant.

Fair rent: The rent determined by a rent officer (or a rent assessment committee) under a regulated tenancy.

Financial Services Authority (FSA): www.fsa.gov.uk.

Fixed or ascertainable period: The period of a tenancy or lease must be defined from the outset, stipulating when it is to begin and when or how it is to end. Although the tenancy of a periodic letting can go on indefinitely, either party can terminate it by giving notice to quit, which expires at the end of a relevant week or month, meeting the requirement of certainty that the arrangement will end at some point.

Gearing: How much you borrow as a proportion of an independent valuation of the property or the property portfolio.

Ground rent: Payment by the leaseholder to the freeholder. Low sums are sometimes referred to as a peppercorn rent.

Grounds for possession: Grounds for possession may be cited in possession proceedings against a tenant when a landlord wants to regain possession of his or her property. There are separate grounds for possession relating to assured tenancies and public-sector tenancies. They were laid down in the Housing Act 1988, as amended by the Housing Act 1996. Landlords may also seek possession when it can be demonstrated that a tenant is no longer using the accommodation as his or her principal home.

Guarantor: Someone, often a parent, who agrees to pay the rent for the tenant in case of default.

Harassment: Actions which interfere with the peace or comfort of the tenant, such as violence, threats, or removing access to services. Harassment is a criminal offence under the Protection from Eviction Act 1977.

House in multiple occupation (HMO): Three unrelated people sharing a property's facilities and some communal rooms. Some HMOs must be licensed. The definition of an HMO is different in Scotland.

Housing Benefit: State support covering part or all of the rent payable by someone on a low income. *See also* Local Housing Allowance.

Housing Health and Safety Rating System (HHSRS): Scheme which provides a hazard rating for all residential property. It requires the structures, means of access, outbuildings, gardens and other spaces to be safe and healthy environments for occupants and visitors.

Independent financial adviser (IFA): Someone trained in the complexities of financial management. Always check that anyone you speak to is regulated by the FSA.

Inventory: A list of items in the rented property on your arrival.

Lease: The same as a tenancy, but the term is usually used to indicate that the property is let for a fixed term, such as six months or a certain number of years, while the word 'tenancy' suggests periodic letting from week to week or month to month.

Leasehold: Ownership for a set period, most commonly applied to flats and other shared buildings.

Let as a separate dwelling: The property cannot be let for business purposes, and must be a 'single dwelling' (not, for example, a house converted into several flats – although each of these separate flats could fall within the definition). It must be 'separate', which boils down to whether the tenant regards and treats it as 'home'. For example, a single room could qualify as a dwelling even if the tenant has the right to share other rooms, such as a kitchen or a bathroom. If the facilities are shared with the landlord, the tenancy would then not be seen as an assured or shorthold tenancy because it has a 'resident landlord'.

Licence: If the occupier is only given the right to share the property (for example, with the owner) rather than have exclusive use of a specific part of it, the arrangement would be a licence, not a lease or a tenancy. This is an important point because tenants have far greater statutory legal protection than licensees.

Local Housing Allowance (LHA): a flat-rate Housing Benefit given to people who rent in the private sector.

Long-term let: A fixed-term let (usually of six months) that is for residential use.

National Approved Letting Scheme (NALS): Government-backed accreditation scheme for both letting and letting management agents.

National Inspection Council for Electrical Installation Contracting (NICEIC): Independent consumer safety organisation for the electrical contracting industry.

Non-resident landlords scheme: A scheme for taxing the UK rental income of non-resident landlords in which the tax is deducted by the letting agent or the tenant.

Notice to quit: Properly known as notice requiring repossession but also known as a Section 21 notice as it is issued under Section 21 of the Housing Act 1989, this is notice to a tenant that they must vacate a property at the end of an assured shorthold tenancy agreement.

Ordinary assured tenancy: *See* Assured tenancy.

Registered rent: A maximum rent on a property set by the Rent Service or Rent Assessment Committee (RAC), publicly available on the Rent Register. Registered rents (often known as Fair Rents) apply to regulated tenancies.

Regulated tenancy: A type of tenancy created by the Rent Act 1977 and ended from 15 January 1989 which offers excellent security of tenure and a regulated rent.

Rent-a-Room Scheme: System offering tax relief when you rent out a room in your own house.

Rent Assessment Committee (RAC): Two- or three-strong panel of people with expertise in the property field who can set a legal maximum rent on a property. There are 14 RACs in England and Wales.

Rent officer: Local authority official who deals with Housing Benefit and liaises with the rent service.

Rent Service: Agency which carries out rental valuations, sets fair rent levels and provides other information to local authorities. The Rent Service is part of the Department for Work and Pensions.

Rental yield: The annual rent of a property worked out as a percentage of its capital value or acquisition price.

Reservation fee: A sum of money that may be payable to a letting agency to keep a property on hold while you get hold of a deposit and/or references.

Resident landlord: Landlord living on the same premises as a tenant.

Return on investment: A more detailed analysis of income versus expenditure in order to establish a long-term view of profit on a let property.

Security of tenure: Gives the tenant an indefinite right to stay, unless the landlord has specific grounds for eviction.

Service charges: Payment for maintenance of shared areas, such as hallways, the roof and drains.

Shorthold tenancy: *See* Assured shorthold tenancy.

Short-term let: A furnished let of between one week and three months.

Stamp duty land tax (SDLT): Tax payable on property purchases and on the notification of tenancy agreements.

Subletting: When a tenant lets part or all of a property to another party.

Tenancy: An arrangement with two key requirements: the letting is for a 'fixed or ascertainable period of time' and it grants 'exclusive possession' of the property. Although this is usually in return for rent, such a charge is not legally part of the tenancy.

Tenancy deposit protection schemes: Schemes aiming to keep tenants' deposits safe and to solve disputes over how much the landlord is allowed to keep to cover damage caused during the tenancy.

Turnover: The amount that you earn from rent.

Universal Credit: A new benefit being introduced from 2013 to replace a mix of benefits such as Tax Credits.

Void: Period when a property is unlet.

Yield: How much money your property is earning.

Useful addresses

Accreditation Network UK
155/157 Woodhouse Lane
Leeds LS2 3ED
Tel: 0113 205 3404
www.anuk.org.uk

Association of British Insurers
51 Gresham Street
London EC2V 7HQ
Tel: 020 7600 3333
www.abi.org.uk

The Association of Independent Inventory Clerks (AIIC)
PO Box 1288
West End
Woking
Surrey GU24 9WE
www.theaiic.co.uk

Association of Residential Letting Agents (ARLA)
Arbon House
6 Tournament Court
Edgehill Drive
Warwick CV34 6LG
Tel: 0844 387 0555
www.arla.co.uk

Citizens Advice
Myddelton House
115–123 Pentonville Road
London N1 9LZ
Tel: see your local phone book
www.citizensadvice.org.uk (England and Wales)
www.citizensadvice.co.uk (NI)
www.cas.org.uk (Scotland)

Council for Licensed Conveyancers (CLC)
16 Glebe Road
Chelmsford
Essex CM1 1QG
Tel: 01245 349599
www.conveyancer.org.uk

Council of Mortgage Lenders (CML)
Bush House
North West Wing
London WC2B 4PJ
Tel: 0845 373 6771
www.cml.org.uk/

Gas Safe Register
PO BOX 6804
Basingstoke RG24 4NB
0800 408 5500
www.gassaferegister.co.uk

Department for Business Innovation & Skills
Response Centre
1 Victoria Street
London SW1H 0ET
Tel: 020 7215 5000
www.bis.gov.uk

Department for Work and Pensions (DWP)
Room 112
The Adelphi
1–11 John Adam Street
London WC2N 6HT
Tel: 020 7712 2171
www.dwp.gov.uk

The Deposit Protection Service (DPS)
The Pavilions
Bridgwater Road
Bristol BS99 6AA
Tel: 0844 4727 000
www.depositprotection.com

Designs on Property Ltd
Newland House
The Point
Weaver Road
Lincoln LN6 3QN
Tel: 0845 838 1763
www.designsonproperty.co.uk

Financial Ombudsman Service (FOS)
South Quay Plaza
183 Marsh Wall
London E14 9SR
Tel: 020 7964 1000
www.financialombudsman.org.uk

Financial Services Authority (FSA)
25 The North Colonnade
Canary Wharf
London E14 5HS
Tel: 020 7066 1000
www.fsa.gov.uk

HM Courts & Tribunals Service (HMCTS)
For all case specific enquiries please contact the relevant court or tribunal office
www.justice.gov.uk/about/hmcts

Her Majesty's Revenue & Customs (HMRC)
Stamp Office helpline:
0845 603 0135
www.hmrc.gov.uk

Homecheck
Landmark Information Group
The Smith Centre
The Fairmile
Henley-on-Thames RG9 6AB
Tel: 0844 844 9966
www.homecheck.co.uk

The Housing Rights Service
Middleton Buildings
10-12 High Street
Belfast BT1 2BA
Tel: 028 90245640
www.housingrights.org.uk

The Inventory Manager
Tel: 0844 725 2000
www.theinventorymanager.co.uk

Land and Property Services
1st Floor
Lincoln Building
27-45 Great Victoria Street
Malone Lower
Belfast BT2 7SL
Tel: 028 9025 1515
www.dfpni.gov.uk/index/land-and-property.htm

Landlordzone
Parkmatic Publications Limited
2 Moor Way
Hawkshaw
Lancashire BL8 4LF
Tel: 0845 260 4420
www.landlordzone.co.uk

Law Society of England and Wales
113 Chancery Lane
London WC2A 1PL
Tel: 020 7242 1222
www.lawsociety.org.uk

Law Society of Ireland
Blackhall Place
Dublin 7
Tel: 0353 1672 4800
www.lawsociety.ie

Law Society of Northern Ireland
Law Society House
98 Victoria Street
Belfast BT1 3GN
Tel: 028 90 231614
www.lawsoc-ni.org

Law Society of Scotland
26 Drumsheugh Gardens
Edinburgh EH3 7YR
Tel: 0131 226 7411
www.lawscot.org.uk

Legal Services Ombudsman
3rd Floor, Sunlight House
Quay Street
Manchester M33JZ
Tel: 0845 601 0794
www.olso.org

mydeposits
Ground Floor, Kingmaker House
Station Road
New Barnet
Hertfordshire EN5 1NZ
Tel: 0844 980 0290
www.mydeposits.co.uk

National Approved Letting Scheme
Tavistock House
5 Rodney Road
Cheltenham GL50 1HX
Tel: 01242 581712
www.nalscheme.co.uk

National Association of Estate Agents (NAEA)
Arbon House
6 Tournament Court
Edgehill Drive
Warwick CV34 6LG
Tel: 0844 387 0555
www.naea.co.uk

National Inspection Council for Electrical Installation Contracting (NICEIC)
Warwick House
Houghton Hall Park
Houghton Regis
Dunstable
Bedfordshire LU5 5ZX
Tel: 0870 013 0382
www.niceic.org.uk

National Landlords Association (NLA)
22–26 Albert Embankment
London SE1 7TJ
Tel: 020 7840 8900
www.landlords.org.uk

Northern Ireland Federation of Housing Associations
6c Citylink Business Park
Albert Street
Belfast BT12 4HB
Tel: 028 9023 0446
www.nifha.org

Northern Ireland Ombudsman
Freepost BEL 1478
Belfast BT1 6BR
Tel: 0800 34 34 24
www.ni-ombudsman.org.uk

The Office of Fair Trading (OFT)
Fleetbank House
2–6 Salisbury Square
London EC4Y 8JX
Tel: 020 7211 8000
Consumer helpline: 0845 7224499
www.oft.gov.uk

OneSearch
1st Floor, Skypark SP1
8 Elliot Place
Glasgow G3 8EP
Tel: 0800 052 0117
www.surveysonline.co.uk

Rentchecks.com
Creditas Ltd
Church House
102 Pendlebury Road
Swinton M27 4BF
Tel: 0844 412 7752
www.rentchecks.com

Residential Landlords Association (RLA)
1 Roebuck Lane
Sale
Manchester M33 7SY
Tel: 0161 962 0010 or 0845 666 5000
www.rla.org.uk

Royal Institution of Chartered Surveyors (RICS)
Parliament Square
London SW1P 3AD
Tel: 0870 333 1600
www.rics.org

Scottish Association of Landlords
20 Forth Street
Edinburgh EH1 3LH
Tel: 0131 270 4774
www.scottishlandlords.com

Scottish Federation of Housing Associations
Pegasus House
375 West George Street
Glasgow G2 4LW
Tel: 0141 332 8113
www.sfha.co.uk

Scottish Legal Services Ombudsman
The Stamp Office
10–14 Waterloo Place
Edinburgh EH1 3EG
Tel: 0131 528 5111
www.slso.org.uk

Shelter
88 Old Street
London EC1V 9HU
Tel: 0808 800 4444
http://england.shelter.org.uk

The Tenancy Deposit Scheme
The Dispute Service Ltd
PO Box 1255
Hemel Hempstead
Herts HP1 9GN
Tel: 0845 226 7837
www.thedisputeservice.co.uk

Tenant Verify
Parkmatic Publications Limited
2 Moor Way
Hawkshaw
Lancashire BL8 4LF
Tel: 0845 260 4421
www.tenantverify.co.uk

UK Association of Letting Agents (UKALA)
PO Box 10582
Colchester
CO1 9JD
Tel: 01206 765456
www.ukala.org.uk

Property websites
www.eigroup.co.uk
www.heritage.co.uk
www.houseweb.co.uk
www.myhouseprice.com
www.ourproperty.co.uk
www.periodproperty.co.uk
www.primelocation.com
www.propertybroker.co.uk
www.propertychecklists.co.uk
www.propertynews.com (for Northern Ireland and Ireland)
www.rightmove.co.uk
www.zoopla.com

Websites dealing with property-related money and legal issues
http://wales.gov.uk/topics/housingandcommunity/housing/ (housing news in Wales)
www.betterrentingscotland.com (general advice on renting in Scotland)
www.communitylegaladvice.org.uk (Community Legal Advice)
www.gov.uk (directory of public services)
www.housingcorp.co.uk (portal for social housing)
www.landlordlaw.co.uk (legal documents online shop)
www.landlordregistrationscotland.gov.uk (information on the Landlord Register in Scotland)
www.landreg.gov.uk (registers title to land in England and Wales)
www.lawscot.org.uk (details of local solicitors in Scotland)
www.lease-advice.org (Leasehold Advisory Service)
www.letsure.co.uk (has links to specialist insurers)
www.lloydsbankinggroup.com/media1/research/house_price_calculator_page.asp (Halifax/ Lloyds House Price Index)
www.moneynet.co.uk (finance comparisons)
www.nationwide.co.uk/hpi (Nationwide house price index)
www.rooms.co.uk (shared ownership information in Scotland and England)
www.scotland.gov.uk/Topics/Housing/Housing (all aspects of housing in Scotland)
www.tradingstandards.gov.uk (consumer protection information)

Index

About Which?

Which? is the largest independent consumer organisation in the UK. A not-for-profit organisation, we exist to make individuals as powerful as the organisations they deal with in everyday life. Our campaigns make people's lives fairer, simpler and safer. The next few pages give you a taster of our many products and services.

For more information, log onto www.which.co.uk or call 01992 822800.

Which? Online and Which? Local

www.which.co.uk is updated regularly, so you can read hundreds of product reports and Best Buy recommendations, keep up to date with Which? campaigns, compare products, use our financial planning tools and search for the best cars on the market. As a Which? member you can sign up to Which? Local, a website of 110,000 local business reviews created for Which? members, by Which? members. Covering everything from plumbers to plasterers and butchers to bakers, our independent member reviews will help you find the best service that won't charge you over the odds. To subscribe, go to www.which.co.uk.

Which? Legal Service

Which? Legal Service offers convenient access to first-class legal advice at unrivalled value. One low-cost annual subscription enables members to receive tailor-made legal advice by telephone or email on a wide variety of legal topics, including consumer law – problems with goods and services, employment law (for employees), holiday problems, neighbour disputes, parking tickets and Wills and Probate Administration in England and Wales. To subscribe, call the Members' helpline: 01992 822828 or go to www.whichlegalservice.co.uk.

Which? Money

Whether you want to boost your pension, make your savings work harder or simply need to find the best credit card, *Which? Money* has the information you need. *Which? Money* offers you honest, unbiased reviews of the best (and worst) personal finance deals, from bank accounts to loans, credit cards to savings accounts. It's also packed with investigations, revealing the truth behind the small print. As a Which? member you also have access to the Which? Money helpline offering free one-to-one guidance on any financial matter. To subscribe, go to www.which.co.uk/money-subscription.

Other Which? books

Which? Books provide impartial, expert advice on everyday matters from finance and law to gardening, property and major life events. We also publish the country's most trusted restaurant guide, *The Good Food Guide*. To find out more about Which? Books, log on to **www.which.co.uk/books** or call **01992 822800**.

Buy, Sell & Move House

Kate Faulkner

ISBN 978 1 84490 142 5

Price £10.99

Buy, Sell and Move House covers the complete buying and selling process, from understanding the market and choosing a mortgage through to completing the sale. Now updated to cover the Government's new housing strategy, the book is packed with expert advice, case studies and top tips.

Develop Your Property

Kate Faulkner

ISBN 978 1 84490 038 1

Price £10.99

Develop Your Property helps add value to your property by guiding you through the processes of extension, renovation and conversion. Learn how to budget and project-manage building work and implement key property changes that can add real value. Includes valuable information on planning permission, building regulations and getting the builders in.

Tax Handbook 2012-13

Tony Levene

ISBN 978 1 84490 132 6

Price £10.99

Fully updated in line with the 2012 Budget, *Tax Handbook 2012–13* is essential reading for all tax payers. Jargon-busting advice explains how to complete a tax return and online assessment, check a tax code and National Insurance, and reduce Inheritance Tax or minimise Capital Gains Tax. This essential guide also demystifies Tax Credits and tax-free perks at work.

Growing Your Own Vegetables Made Easy

ISBN 978 1 84490 128 9

Price £10.99

From carrots to courgettes, learn how to cultivate your favourite produce with *Growing Your Own Vegetables Made Easy*. Compiled by the Which? Gardening experts, the book shows you how to sow, grow and harvest a wide range of vegetables, and also features advice on preventing and controlling pests and diseases.

The Gardener's Year Made Easy

ISBN 978 1 84490 120 3

Price £10.99

Whether you want to care for your borders or tend your vegetable plot, *The Gardener's Year Made Easy* guides you through the essential garden tasks month by month. Showing you what to do and when, this practical handbook sets out the tasks to complete each month to keep your garden in tip top shape. The book includes advice on lawns, borders, fruit and vegetables as well as the pests and diseases to look out for.

'Which? tackles the issues that really matter to consumers and gives you the advice and active support you need to buy the right products.'